MIRACLE ON THE SALT RIVER

Water, Family & Farming in the Arizona Desert

Meredith Haley Whiteley

THE
History
PRESS

Published by The History Press
Charleston, SC 29403
www.historypress.net

Front cover: Joe and Ollie Haley, circa 1940. *Courtesy of the author.*
Back cover: The Roosevelt Dam dedication, March 18, 1911. *Courtesy of the Tempe History Museum.* Ollie Haley and her children. *Courtesy of the author.*

First published 2014

Manufactured in the United States

ISBN 978.1.62619.694.0

Library of Congress CIP data applied for.

In Memory of
Joe Haley Jr.

Contents

ACKNOWLEDGEMENTS

This book came together over a long period of time. I am grateful to everyone here: Carol St. Clair and the Glendale Arizona Historical Society; Jared Smith and the Tempe History Museum; Arizona State Archives; Casa Grande Valley Historical Society Museum; Arizona Baptist Historical Commission Archive; First Baptist Church, Glendale; The Salt River Project; Alberta Threewit; Ruth Wilkinson; and Brenda McClurkin. Unfortunately, many wonderful and helpful people have died in the meantime: Ada Fern Goodman, LouEdna McAllister, Genevieve Hannah, Dorothy Doyle, Della Card and Carl Abel. Most especially, thank you to Joe Haley Jr. (deceased), Felicity and Michael Seth, Marcia Melton and Wes Whiteley.

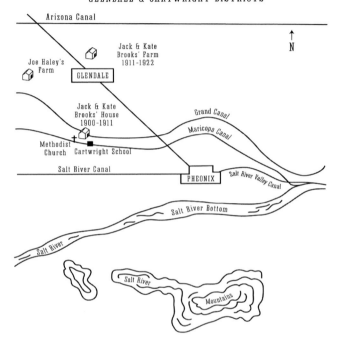

GLENDALE & CARTWRIGHT DISTRICTS

Arizona Canal

N

Joe Haley's Farm

GLENDALE

Jack & Kate Brooks' Farm 1911-1922

Jack & Kate Brooks' House 1900-1911

Grand Canal

Maricopa Canal

Methodist Church

Cartwright School

Salt River Canal

PHEONIX

Salt River Valley Canal

Salt River Bottom

Salt River

Salt River Mountains

A map of the Salt River Valley.

1

REDEEMING THE DESERT

Drought toyed with the American desert on the eve of the twentieth century. It manipulated land, fortunes and lives as if Drought had its own mind, conniving and powerful. Skies blazed white-hot in summer. Snow barely dusted mountains those last winters of the old century, sending scant runoff into thirsty desert creeks and rivers, like Arizona's Salt River. Low water flow meant consternation in the Salt River Valley where farmers looked to river-fed canals to feed their fields and livelihoods. Drought was just beginning.[1]

The dust rolled in then, so thick a man couldn't see a foot ahead. Lightning followed close behind, exploding better than the Fourth of July. Hard, pelting rain fell, washing away men's fear. Most were quick to forget Drought, except old-timers—grizzled loners more at ease with the desert than anyone else. Several of the old men tried to sound the alarm, saying that Drought would come again, with more ferocity. No one listened. The last thing rich, powerful men of the Salt River Valley wanted was negative talk. Bankers, real estate developers and others wanting to boss the Valley knew word about water troubles would send all the Midwest farmers and New York investors with money to burn someplace else in a hurry. Farmers who had already invested everything they had couldn't bear hearing bad news.[2]

The old men were right, of course. Denial became harder for investors and new farmers alike as the dry spells lasted longer. Drought talk in the Salt River Valley grew desperate as farmers watched water trickle to nothing in their ditches. Neighbors shot and killed neighbors over nothing more than a few hours' run of the ditch.

The problem wasn't just the amount of water flowing into the ditches but the condition of the ditches themselves. Drought on the Salt River watershed cut into canal company profits, driving investors to tighten the budgets for repairs. Broken, choked canals sent what precious water there was spilling out before it reached farmers. It was an old dance: East versus West, corporations versus farmers, but this time the jig spun out in uncharted steps, changing the face of the West.

Not all were losers. Occasional rains and a good water table in alfalfa fields north of the Salt River supported five or six cuttings of alfalfa hay a year in nearby fields. Farmers on the Maricopa Canal, like Bruce Brooks, stood to make a small killing.[3]

Bruce was a newcomer to the Valley. Times were bad in Kentucky, and across most of the nation, when he arrived in 1898, penniless. Otherwise, he wouldn't leave his wife, Margaret, and four young girls.[4]

He bunked initially with his sister, Pearl, and her husband. She'd badgered both brothers, Bruce and Jack, to move to the Valley. Like many, Pearl and her husband were driven to the Salt River Valley by tuberculosis. It would be years still, before the discovery of the tuberculosis bacillus and implementation of effective treatment. Until then, dry air was the conventional prescription for a disease that remained one of the country's leading killers. Testimonials—like the one broadly circulated of a sufferer from Los Angeles who was at death's door and made instantly well in the "marvelous climate" of the Salt River Valley—gave the dying and their families tangible hope. Hope and miracles: those suffering clung tenaciously to both. They had little else.[5]

Pearl and her husband bought sixty acres of improved land in the Cartwright District, six miles west of Phoenix and four miles north of the Salt River. Over five hundred people lived within the six by six mile area, the largest portion children. Neighbors came from all over the nation, many moving a few times before landing in the district.[6]

Pearl's land came with a good adobe house and deeded water rights on the Maricopa Canal. There were eight other canals siphoning water off the Salt River as it flowed south, then west across the wide desert floor. Most followed the tracks of canals built hundreds of years earlier by the Hohokam Indians. Three canals, the Grand, Salt River and Maricopa, drew north of the westward flowing river. Five canals drew from the south. The newest canal, the Arizona, drew further north, feeding vast acreage across the northwest.[7]

The Salt River Valley's water arena was contentious from the moment settlers began cleaning out the old canals. The primary battle pitted farmers against canal company owners and investors. Dissension started right out of the gate, when investors filed claims for almost seven million acre-feet of water per year, five and one-half times the normal flow of the river. Most of these were "floating rights," often owned by eastern investors for speculative purposes. Fortunately, Pearl and her husband bought deeded rights. Not all of the farmers were so lucky.

Farmers said early on that the Valley's irrigation system was overextended and the day of reckoning would come when smaller farmers without deeded rights were cut off. Defending their future, a mob of local farmers tore out a dam built on the new Grand Canal in 1878. Their action had no effect. Investors and developers kept right on building. A few years later, the Arizona Canal Company constructed forty-four miles of new canal, opening up another 100,000 acres to potential cultivation. The company also formed an improvement company and built a six-mile "Grand Avenue" slicing diagonally northwest from the heart of Phoenix toward

The Arizona Canal. Note lush vegetation along the canal. Photographer unknown, n.d. *Courtesy of the Library of Congress, Prints & Photographs Division, HAER ARIZ, 7-phen.v, 1—11.*

Excavation work in the Arizona Canal. Camelback Mountain is in the distance.
Photographer: Walter J. Lubken, n.d. *Courtesy of the Library of Congress, Prints & Photographs Division, HAER ARIZ, 7-phen.v, 1—4.*

the new planned villages of Glendale and Peoria. More threatening for local farmers, the company bought controlling interest in the Salt River, Grand and Maricopa Canals so that it controlled most of the water on the north side of the river. The company failed shortly after, reorganizing as the Arizona Water Company.[8]

Water turned the dry, fertile Salt River Valley into an oasis capable of supporting the commercial growth of peach and pear orchards, grapes, citrus, berries, melons, vegetables, olives, figs, sorghum, grains and dairy. Alfalfa hay eclipsed everything else, however. Cattlemen around the Valley, in the mountains to the north and all over southern California and parts of western Texas could not get enough.[9]

Bruce's brother, Jack, was still back in Kentucky, playing the horses more than usual since he had no work. He and Bruce married sisters Kate and Margaret. Both women were faithful to the Methodist Episcopal Church, South and hated liquor and gambling. Jack drank and gambled. The sisters nagged and worked to find Jack a better way to spend his time.

One thing was for certain: Jack had no intention of moving to Arizona or anywhere else. Bruce had been more realistic. He knew they were at the end of their rope in Kentucky. He and Margaret scraped together enough for one train fare.

Arriving in Phoenix, Bruce picked up day labor jobs cutting weeds with a scythe along Central Avenue. The town was abuzz with talk of the Rough Riders and local boys biting the dust in far off Cuba, but Bruce focused on getting work and saving every penny. He soon moved up the pay scale and joined haying and threshing crews working west of town.

Bruce never let his wooden leg get in the way of his ambition. He lost the leg at age eleven after his gun accidentally discharged while he hunted with friends. Six months after arriving in the Salt River Valley, Bruce had enough saved to rent a two-room house and send for Margaret. The new place wasn't much, but he'd worked hard to get it in shape. Evenings were still hot, so Bruce set the beds out in the yard, covering them with yards of new mosquito netting, before driving a borrowed spring wagon to meet the train that night.

Frazzled, Margaret and the girls disembarked at Albuquerque to change trains. Grooming the girls in the lounge, Margaret struck up a conversation with a friendly woman. The two soon discovered they would be neighbors in the Cartwright District.

With only twenty thousand people in 1900, the Salt River Valley was a small world. It got significantly smaller during the summer. Anyone

The Grand Canal reconstruction, near the Salt River, looking east toward Tempe Butte, n.d. *Courtesy of the Library of Congress, Prints & Photographs Division, HAER ARIZ,7-TEMP,8—7.*

with money exited the Valley, to the coast cities of California, or the new summer colony in Flagstaff. Newspapers and the Salt River Valley Board of Trade tried to discourage the exodus, saying that dry heat isn't hot. Those who stayed in the Valley through the summer knew that was a lie.[10]

The sky was a blaze of bright stars as Bruce's family headed from the station to their new home. Everyone fell into bed once they reached the house. Bruce left for work before dawn. There was little time for Margaret and her husband to talk, but one thing Bruce made clear before leaving: water had different rules in the desert. He hauled the large canteens of drinking and cooking water in on horseback. Water for everything else ran in the ditch.

Sitting on the steps early the next morning, Margaret surveyed her surroundings. The September morning was already warm. Margaret spent a while listening to the joyful squeals of the four girls at play in the dirt yard, no more than chicken scratch. Like most children, her girls were happy almost anywhere, as long as they were no longer cooped up.

Looking around, she saw only the tall gray-green tamarisks lining the ditch and shielding the house and yard to the south and west. They were ugly but crucial when the hot afternoon sun blasted the little wood house, which had no insulation. Christy Road, a major east-west thoroughfare, ran in front, a narrow dirt ditch next to it. Another road followed north and south beyond the trees to the west. The full ditches gleamed with water, beckoning Margaret to explore.

Walking to one, she discovered the banks covered with dry, prickly Johnson grass. Dark water flowed swiftly below. Standing upright, Margaret scanned the horizon. She saw mountains in every direction.

Inside the house sat a mound of dirty white dresses, bloomers and diapers. Margaret faced more than just dirty water that morning. Even if she solved the water problem, she still didn't know how to do laundry, clean water or not. There was always someone in Kentucky to do laundry for her. Bruce had warned that the burden would be on her. She knew she was going to have to work harder if she and Bruce ever had a chance of buying their own land. That first day in the Valley was Margaret's day of reckoning.

She stared at the dirty clothes, the house and the yard, and then picked up the pails to work on the water as best she could. Making her way through the weeds, Margaret lowered the pail. What she brought up was dirtier than she had imagined. The finality of the move to Arizona hit her. She stumbled to the step, tears spilling down her face. Quickly, the four girls surrounded their mother, stroking her hair and wiping the tears.

As she sat with her girls, Margaret figured out how to let the sediment settle and skim the ditch water until it was clear enough for her white wash. She skimmed and scrubbed in a duet of letting go and moving forward until her hands were raw and her eyes cried out. Years later, determined to put her own spin on that day and those that followed, Margaret told her daughters that she got through those early days by finding within herself a well of strength and ingenuity she didn't yet know she had. A woman couldn't get by in the desert without it.

Margaret and the younger girls walked Nannie the mile to the brick schoolhouse a few days later. The school enrolled seventy-nine. Six-year-old Nannie was in the primary class, with a female teacher. Older students had the stern male "Professor." All grades shared the library's twenty-five volumes. The school had no water supply until parents built a cistern a couple of years later, so students either brought water or drank directly from the ditch. The school building served as church, center of the community and water-dispute meeting center.[11]

Bruce was an engine. He soon moved the family to a better house—with well water—just a mile west of the schoolhouse. As importantly, he laid plans to start his own hay-baling business. Hay cutting and baling in the Valley in 1899 was a sure bet if the man running the business could keep the horses alive, the wagon going and find labor. Every winter, cattlemen sent thousands of head of cattle down to the Valley from higher Arizona elevations and West Texas to fatten them up and ship to slaughterhouses. Drought taking its toll, cattlemen sent cattle to the Valley early, buying more feed at higher prices.[12]

Finding and keeping labor was the biggest problem. With Arizona's mines booming, men could make more as laborers at the Copper Queen or United Verde mines than any farmer in the Valley was willing to pay. With little labor available, hay farmers worked past dark, putting their wives and children to work. There was money in hay, though, if a man and his family were willing to work. One story told about a teacher from the Cartwright school who, just three years earlier, took $400 he saved and rented an 80-acre alfalfa farm five miles north of Phoenix. The man quickly earned enough on his venture to put money down on 160 acres in the same district. The former teacher made a real go of his place with just one field hand and his own dawn-to-dark labor. Bruce bought a good team and wagon and started hunting for a crew other than his wife and small girls. He would work and save for his own property.[13]

Bruce wasn't in the hay business long before his sister Pearl came to him with a proposal. The desert cure failed her husband. He and Pearl were leaving immediately and wanted Bruce and Margaret to take over the farm. Bruce and Margaret took the offer with mixed emotions. They moved into the four-room adobe house immediately. They were barely settled before life was upset again. Pearl, their youngest, died of scarlet fever.[14]

Margaret's sorrow was the nudge that brought Jack and Kate to Arizona the following March. They arrived in the middle of a record-breaking heat wave with their three girls: Fannie, age five; Rebecca, age four; and Marguritte, eighteen months. Kate was also pregnant. Margaret and Bruce provided a place to stay, clean water and an introduction to friends and church. Bruce hired Jack to work in his hay business.

Demand for hay grew. Bruce hired as many men as he could find to cut and bale, putting Margaret and Kate to work operating the mobile "cook shack" he built. Good, abundant food kept his crews going sun up through sun down. When Kate gave birth to her fourth girl, Ollie, she put the baby in a basket covered with mosquito netting under shade just outside the shack. The other girls played contentedly close by. Both sisters always had control of their children.

The home Jack and Kate finally rented was a two-room shack with no water except the Grand Canal flowing right outside the door. It wasn't supposed to be this way for Kate. She'd heard her sister's tale of arriving to nothing but a shack and having to do laundry with dirty ditch water, but Kate was sure Bruce and Margaret would help them avoid that hardship.

While Margaret's four-room adobe was modest compared to what she and Kate grew up with, it was luxury next to Kate's new home. Women around the neighborhood told Kate that they, too, lived in small shacks when they first arrived. Housing standards were often low for those putting most of their money into buying property and equipment. The women were full of suggestions for living in the small house, telling Kate to have the wood stove and beds moved into the yard nine months out of the year and do all bathing in the canal. Kate politely listened and followed some of the suggestions, but she had no intention of living in that shack long enough to move the beds and stove outdoors. She would push and prod Jack in every way in her power until he got them out of there!

The differences between the two Brooks brothers went far beyond Jack's dark and Bruce's blond looks. Jack was passive, until it came to Bruce bossing him. It was only a matter of time before the two parted ways. With the big demand for farm labor in the West Valley, Jack didn't find it difficult to get additional work. His problem wasn't making money in Arizona. It was holding on to it.

The brothers remained close once they no longer worked side by side. They joined the flood of farmers, from both sides of the river, gathered in the ornate opera house one early September morning. Everyone had come to hear talk of building a storage dam in the mountains above the Salt River Valley. Drought and its accompanying pressures nurtured the idea. A dam, people said, would hold the excess runoff when snowfall was plentiful so that farmers in the Valley below would have something in the lean years. The system would also ration the amount of water coming down the canals, making sure everyone got their allotment and eliminating floods. Few debated the potential value of a dam. Funding and direction were the questions.[15]

Chairman McGowan got the meeting rolling.[16]

> *Ten years ago, when I came first to this territory, I was told that the Salt River Valley was the garden spot of the universe, that it was the vale of wondrous gifts and opportunities: that all it lacked to make its people corpulent with prosperity was a reservoir...But you all know how it has been.*
>
> *And I want to tell you, gentlemen, that if all the curses that have been uttered since the fall of man could be gathered at Tonto Basin today. If they could be piled one on another by the hands of the reckless ones who have so laboriously dug them from the quarries of hell, if they could be cemented there with all the lies that have been told, all the deceit and malice and envy and sin that have been conceived since the beginning of time, we would have a pile that would reach to heaven and be a monument throughout eternity to man's depravity, but we would not have a dam nor a reservoir. Now how may we best secure water storage?*

McGowan told the farmers crammed into the Opera House in Phoenix that September morning that greed and malice were the villains.

The heat in the room became unbearable. Someone moved that all speeches be limited to ten minutes, but others declared they didn't leave their fields not to have their complete say. One man came only to tell the others it was a fact that a dam on the Salt River was a physical impossibility. Another countered that not only was a dam on the Salt possible, but he heard they could bring water all the way to the Salt River Valley from the Colorado River too!

"If the old fogies of France, Italy and Egypt can build a dam on the Nile, our genius Yankees can surely accomplish it on the Salt!" another proclaimed.

Men from Buckeye, at the end of the irrigation line and watching their stock die of thirst, begged not to be left out of plans.

Most of those in the hot opera house that day came to hear what Ben Fowler, a member of the National Irrigation Association and West Valley farmer, knew. Dwight Heard, a Phoenix attorney with a high interest in taking the lead on the dam project, seemed to be there to counter everything Fowler said.

The afternoon debate settled down to an argument between Fowler and Heard. Fowler was convinced that the federal government could and would build the dam, but garnering that support would take a concerted effort by Valley farmers.

Dwight Heard spoke after Fowler. He believed the federal government would not fund a dam on the Salt River soon enough to relieve the problems of farmers in the Valley. Instead, Heard pushed for Congressional approval that would allow the Salt River Valley to bond itself to build the dam.

Both men agreed on one thing: the escalating conflict between local canal companies and farmers could sink either approach. The farmers' desperation and canal investors' scramble to make a killing showed no signs of easing. Settling conflicts and laying solid ground for the future would be no easy task.[17]

The specter of a federally sponsored dam hardened the canal companies' position. With little or no water to sell as the drought continued, canal companies halted maintenance completely. Ditches and canals filled with weeds, their sides crumbled. Wooden head gates and dam supports rotted in the hot sun.

Farmers clamored in response. Most of the discontent came from farmers on the Maricopa, Salt River and Grand Canals, where the Arizona Water Company owned controlling interest. With water in the river low, company officials divvied out water to their Arizona Canal customers first, shorting the Maricopa, Salt River and Grand Canal customers further downstream.[18]

The summer of 1902 arrived with a vengeance, June temperatures breaking all records. Cattle died across the Southwest. Alfalfa growth was stunted, pasturage nearly exhausted. Fruit trees showed signs of serious damage. Summer rains came but brought little relief. Rain brought, instead, an invasion of large cockroaches. Agriculture experts advised residents to make a paste out of gunpowder and spread it thick around baseboards, keeping children and fire away.[19]

Both Brooks families were more fortunate than many. Farming so close to the river, Bruce was able to get enough water to seed his alfalfa. The high water table on his land sustained crop growth and gave him a precious commodity during a time of low supply. Jack milked half a dozen cows, feeding them on his twenty acres of pasturage when he could get water from the Grand Canal, moving them to other pasturage when water was short.

Debate continued on how to fund a dam, until one day, when government surveyors swarmed Phoenix, buying supplies. It appeared someone had made a decision. Then George H. Maxwell, president of the National Irrigation Association, stepped off the train. Everyone knew he had the power. Standing under the August afternoon sun, Maxwell surprised a crowd of over one thousand when he said that the dam would be built to benefit farmers only, not canal companies. In addition, the dam would provide power for the profitable copper mining operations in nearby mountains.[20]

Maxwell went on to say that all the parties had to settle their differences, and quickly, if the project was going to work. Given the history, it wasn't unreasonable for canal company officials to think the "harmony" requirement a naïve joke that turned the project in their favor. Almost immediately, Judge Joseph Kibbey of the Arizona Territorial Supreme Court went to work on the bones of an organizational concept to give farmers a way to pay the government back for the estimated $2.5 million in construction costs and take over administration of water storage and distribution once the dam was completed. Key to Judge Kibbey's work was the decision that canal companies could no longer hold the project hostage. Dam construction could begin before the sale of canals. Haggling over funding and ownership took another year. Finally, construction of the road into the rugged site for the dam began in mid-1903. Building the road to the site was an engineering feat in and of itself. Officials estimated it would take four to five years to finish the dam. Jack, Bruce and other farmers had crops, bills and stubborn canal companies to contend with in the meantime.[21]

The spring and early summer of 1903 were mild. Another big flood rolled down the Salt River in April, this time damaging Southside canals. The moisture revived thirsty fields. More rain in mid-June pushed the third crop of alfalfa and saved melons and fruits. Summer storms hit in late July, bringing relief. Everyone was ready to declare the drought over.[22]

Construction on the dam put the Valley's development train on the move again. Ongoing efforts to bring the sugar-beet industry to the Valley succeeded in early 1903. The Glendale plant was to be built of bricks made on site and use water siphoned from the now-almost-dry Arizona Canal. Betting that the worst of the drought was over, developers encouraged farmers to plant beets immediately for the next season. It didn't rain for nine months.[23]

Valley thermometers registered ninety-six by early April 1904 and kept climbing. Crops planted in the fall of 1903 never sprouted. Alfalfa planted that winter was light; the second and third crops never appeared. Range cattle lost flesh rapidly. By early July, cattlemen fed their stock mesquite beans and faced losses in the millions. Many farmers and stockmen pulled out. "Dry Weather Bargains" could be bought for a song.[24]

Jack and Bruce both scrambled to stay afloat. Their salvation was their dairy businesses, but feed was difficult to get. Jack had trouble making rent and had nothing to water his field. The Grand Canal was bone dry.

"At Last!" blazed the headlines the morning of July 22. Summer showers finally arrived. The glorious rain was renewal to the people of the Salt River Valley. They danced bareheaded and soaked to the skin in the streets and on their parched yards. As good as the rain felt, however, the celebration was premature. Northside canals were in terrible shape and could not handle

The Glendale Sugar Beet Factory, n.d. *Courtesy of the Glendale Arizona Historical Society.*

the water. Aside from the rain, farmers got nothing. With anger fueled by frustration and worry, they organized a protective association and sent representatives to the Arizona Water Company, demanding the company repair the canals immediately.[25]

"I'll refer the matter to the company's directors," the water company manager replied in the face of the farmers' representatives.

"The hell you will," one man shouted.

Another representative urged calm reason. Writing and waiting for permission took too long, he told the manager. The farmers had no time to wait. There were men and teams ready to work on clearing and repairing the canals. They just needed the manager's command.

"Two men followed the Grand Canal last evening to find out why they weren't getting any water," another representative reported. "What they found was nearly nine feet of checks along the canal. At the head of the canal they found a man who said he was stationed by the company manager to allow only a small amount of water into the Grand Canal and the remainder of the water was turned away! The man said he had his orders and had to obey them!"

A deep, calmer voice could be heard amidst the anger and shouting. "Look," the man began, "we demand that you get crews out there now and start fixing those canals."

"I can't do that," the company manager replied. "Not without direct authorization from my directors. Like I said, I will refer the matter to them. Good day gentlemen."

"You lily livered jack ass," someone belted out.

That was enough for the company manager. He punched the farmer in the face.

It was time to leave the canal companies behind. West Valley farmers were digging within days of that meeting. They called their new canal the Appropriators Canal and funded it with $50,000 contributed by desperate farmers. Just about everyone in the lower West Valley farming neighborhood bought a stake.[26]

The next flood rolled down the Salt before the new canal could handle the water. The rains kept coming. Water spread everywhere, was dangerous, but useless for desperate farmers. The Appropriators kept digging. The river became a raging torrent again in late August, slowing construction on the new canal. The entire Southwest flooded in October, tying up trains and mail and downing Western Union lines for days. Travelers from the east could access the Valley only by detouring west through Los Angeles. Rains in

Flood-damaged head gate to Grand Canal. The Phoenix Railroad bridge was damaged by the March 1905 flood. *Courtesy of the Tempe History Museum.*

January carried away the tuberculars' tent city near the new capital building, just west of downtown Phoenix. The Salt River spread out a mile wide in some spots, taking good top soil with it all the way to the Colorado River and down to the sea. Cave Creek, north of the Valley, flooded in February and March, wiping out parts of Glendale.[27]

The drought was officially over. Rains and flooding that came in early April tore apart the heads for the canal system, further paralyzing it. The Maricopa and Salt River Canals got some water through an old joint head, but water users like Jack on the Grand Canal were without a source. The Appropriators' proposal to Grand Canal directors that they be allowed to connect the Appropriators Canal with the Grand Canal was quickly turned down. Farmers on the Grand Canal turned their back on canal owners, asking the Appropriators to extend their canal further west, right next to the now dry Grand. Grand Canal farmers quickly purchased stock in the Appropriators to make sure the extension could happen.[28]

The Arizona Water Company filed suit to stop the construction, claiming the Appropriators crossed a piece of Arizona Water Company property. The Appropriators crew kept digging as its directors filed to have the land in question condemned. The judge refused the injunction and ruled in favor of the Appropriators's condemnation question. The new canal stretched thirty miles and irrigated 38,000 acres. Fifteen thousand of those acres could receive water from no other source. Unfortunately, it could not reach desperate farmers uphill under the now dry Arizona Canal.[29]

Jack Brooks and others just like him built the Appropriators Canal with not much more than their bare hands. Though Jack didn't own land, problems with canal companies were as much his as they were anyone's. He was ready with his wagon and team from the first dig until the canal finished, just two miles short of his home, right on the banks of the Grand Canal.

The canal brought the neighborhood back to life. Hay and pasturage were again plentiful. Jack was in the right business at the right time. The Valley's population continued to grow and demand for milk and butter outstripped supply. Alfalfa was "in the clover." Mining in the mountains around the Valley stayed strong, pushing much of that demand. The health industry also drove growth in the Valley. Investors built a number of sanitariums around the Valley. Most health seekers, however, still lived in poverty on their own.[30]

Pundits warned Valley residents not to get too heady with the new prosperity, but it was difficult to take the advice after such a long dreary spell. Bruce and Margaret looked to expand. They bought 160 acres of unimproved land further west of their farm and began clearing off native vegetation in their "spare" time.

Remains of the original Arizona Canal head, looking east. Photographer: Mark Durben, December 1990. *Courtesy of the Library of Congress, Prints & Photographs Division, HAER ARIZ,7-phen.v,1—33.*

The Valley water scene was relatively peaceful in 1906. Work went slowly on the dam. Contract disputes over cement and the road, floods and engineering problems all brought delays and increased costs. The Water Users' Association remained officially optimistic and busy. Their immediate objective was buying the canals.

Arizona Water Company investors set the value of their holdings in the Arizona, Grand, Maricopa and Salt River Valley canals at $1.5 million. Proof that the farmers could build a parallel canal for a figure under $100,000 undermined the claim. Weakening the investors' position more was the fact that the Arizona Water Company was on weak financial ground and just about everyone knew it. Repair of the head gate supplying water to the Arizona Canal was costly and not going well. In the meantime, the few remaining farmers on the Arizona Canal grew more desperate without irrigation. Almost everyone around Glendale and Peoria had moved on.

Ben Fowler handled the canal purchase negotiations for the Water Users'. He tried to convince the Arizona Water Company that their investment was

The Roosevelt Dam under construction. Photographer: Walter J. Lubken, circa 1908. *Courtesy of the Salt River Project.*

The Roosevelt Dam reservoir, n.d. *Courtesy of the National Archives, photo number 294696.*

worth $200,000, at best. In the process, the Arizona Water Company went into receivership. The deal was done in June 1906. The government bought the four Northside canals for $235,000, with the farmer-owned Salt River Valley Water Users' Association promising to pay back the amount in ten years. The four original canal companies were finally out of business. That left the Appropriators. Investors wanted to sell their canal to the government and recoup their investment, but the government showed no interest.[31]

Hopes were high the new ownership would bring immediate relief to farmers who had little or no water. Those hopes were realized in early April when water was turned into the Arizona Canal. Optimism was short lived when heavy rains in July broke the canal in several places, flooding fields at the breaks, denying farmers down the line. The new order showed its mettle, repairing the breaks quickly, building farmer confidence in what was to come.[32]

Valley farmers focused on a new day. They'd outlasted the drought and driven the canal companies out of business. Soon they would be the owners and beneficiaries of the largest reclamation project ever attempted in this country. Not a few had trouble imagining a life in which *water* wasn't their first worry in the morning and last thought at night.

❋ GLENDALE ❋

An advertisement for settlers in Glendale, promising the temperance covenant, circa 1900. *Courtesy of the Glendale Arizona Historical Society.*

2

ABIDING

D rought had no effect on the flow of good Kentucky bourbon in the Salt River Valley. Jack Brooks took his neat at the Alhambra roadhouse on Grand Avenue just north of the place he and Kate rented. "Grand" was certainly a misnomer, as it applied to Grand Avenue after the Arizona Canal dried up and sent all the busted farmers around the planned towns of Glendale and Peoria packing. Still, the roadhouse did a booming business, prospering and expanding every time the pious of Phoenix banned another "evil" within city limits. City men just took their appetites further out, showing up by the dozens at roadhouses outside city limits across the Valley.[33]

Not that people in the Cartwright District had more tolerance than city folks for what went on at the Alhambra roadhouse. Too many neighbors and employees spent time and money there, creating problems throughout the district. It was easy for a man to sink quite a bit of both into the roadhouse's liquor, gambling tables and women, leaving his family scraping for necessities. That wasn't the worst of it. Young boys were fascinated by the place, too. They circled around like hungry dogs looking for bones.

Kate Brooks came to Arizona hoping Jack would mend his ways, but the mounting evidence was too damning. Missing money, absences, lies and the undeniable smell of liquor ultimately broke down her denial. Try as she did, Kate couldn't keep Jack's drinking a secret. It was all she could do to hold her head high around the neighborhood.[34]

The hardest thing for Kate was facing her own sister, Margaret. The money Jack spent at the Alhambra roadhouse would buy a decent house, Kate figured. Instead, Jack seemed content to have his family crammed into nothing more than a shack while Margaret and Bruce had a fine home. When the Grand Canal ran dry, Kate couldn't even bathe her children or wash clothes unless she took everything and everybody to Margaret's. Those were the days when Kate's humiliation was at its worst.

This didn't bother Jack much. He bathed at the roadhouse. Jack was the outgoing type, making friends with each influx of city men. He always got a kick when he ran into one or more of those men at one of the Good Templars temperance meetings around the Valley that he attended with Kate, Margaret and Bruce. The foursome, along with just about everyone else in the Cartwright neighborhood, signed the oath to not touch alcohol, but the Templars' attraction went well beyond temperance crusading. Salt River Valley Templars lodges staged inter-lodge debate competitions on issues of the day, like women's suffrage and statehood.[35]

The lack of a decent house and sober husband drove Kate to social frenzy. She stepped right into Margaret's world her first day in the Valley and never stopped. Like Margaret, Kate joined the interdenominational Sunday school held at the Cartwright school. It was no Methodist Episcopal Church, South assembly like they'd attended back in Kentucky, but each sister adapted, making it the center of her life outside the home. Both sisters rushed off every week to teach children's Sunday school, dragging with them big hampers of food for the dinner that followed the meeting's once-a-month preaching.[36]

Ties to the Sunday schoolhouse meeting defined much of the sisters' week. There were meetings, revivals, socials and trainings for Sunday meeting members, not to mention Cartwright's Ladies' Literary Society, Good Templars, dozens of informal dinners, quilting days and children's parties.

The Sunday fellowship was nowhere near enough for Kate. She soon found Phoenix was no religious backwater, despite its isolation. The famed Dwight L. Moody preached in town in 1899, just months before Kate's arrival. Moody's visit was a spiritual watershed, setting local pastors on fire and putting Phoenix on the national evangelism circuit. The landscape was active for months to come. Conservative and restrained, like Moody, or theatrical, like many of the hell-fire tent preachers, Kate loved them all.[37]

One of the memorable evangelistic meetings was the month-long revival by Dr. E.J. Bulgin at Central Methodist Episcopal Church, South in March 1907. Typical of evangelists of the time, he brought his own choirmaster to lead a local mass choir in the new hymns popular with their audiences. Local churches and newspapers heralded the evangelist's coming for days.[38]

Methodists, Presbyterians, Baptists and almost every other of the Valley's mix of white Protestant denominations and community congregations filled Central Methodist's pews every night of the crusade. Phoenix churches often practiced the cooperative unionism that was sweeping across the country, joining forces for evangelistic meetings, temperance and community charity efforts. Pastors of the city's big Protestant churches made use of "unionism," especially during the hot summer months when they locked up their sanctuaries, left town for cooler places and turned loose what remained of their flocks to attend the "union" services at Eastlake Park on Sunday evenings.[39]

All of Kate's children were scrubbed within an inch of their lives. The four girls, hair tied in their big Sunday-best grosgrain bows, wore Sunday dresses, starched and ironed. Kate had a new dress. She worried she'd gotten the dress too tight in the bust. Thirteen years and seven pregnancies had transformed the perky slender girl Kate once was into a heavy matron way before her time. Her rich brown hair was still thick, but graying rapidly. Her face was now plump and round. Her bosom was heavy, her plump arms barely reaching around. Kate's ankles swelled all the time. The pregnancies and nursing made her so hungry. Years of drought hadn't helped, either. Gardens withered and died, leaving Valley women little alternative but to cook with more flour and fat. Kate didn't break the bad habits much once the rains returned and water flowed back to gardens and fields. Her biscuits, cakes and fudge tasted just as good during better times as they did during the bad.

Jack made sure his family arrived in plenty of time for him and Kate to visit. Parking the newest additions to the family, Henry aged three and Victor aged one, with the older girls in a pew near the front, Kate and Jack circulated among the arriving crowd, renewing friendships.

The choirmaster's warm, rich baritone filled the sanctuary with the lines of the soothing new gospel song, "His Eye Is on the Sparrow."[40]

The music rolled over the audience like waves. Kate could count on her fingers the number of times she sat in a pew and felt the calming peace of a "real" church since she had left Kentucky to come west. Seats at the Cartwright fellowship were school desks, bolted to the floor by a zealot neighbor to squash any notions of dancing in the Cartwright neighborhood's only meeting place. More community gathering than church, Cartwright's Sunday meeting lacked any notion of peace.

The Brooks family, n.d. *Front row, left to right*: Leolia, Victor, Jack. *Middle row*: Henry, Kate, Ollie, Marguritte. *Back row*: Rebecca, Fannie. *Courtesy of the Ruth Wilkinson Collection.*

Finally, the evangelist took the stage, looking solemnly over the expectant crowd. "God has ten yardsticks he measures his children by," he began. "These yardsticks are the Ten Commandments." The sermon spoke directly to every listener's jealousy. Kate couldn't help but think it was directed at her.

No African Americans or Hispanics were in attendance. Religion was segregated in Phoenix. Beginning in 1902, the *Arizona Gazette* listed both the African Methodist Episcopal churches and the white Protestant churches every Saturday. A note later that same year tells of services at the Mexican Methodist Episcopal church, while a line in 1903 says the "old" pastor is returning to First African Church. A Roman Catholic church, mostly attended by Mexican Americans, was built in 1881.[41]

Summer brought the Methodist encampment a few miles northwest of downtown Phoenix. Summer camps gave Margaret, Kate and others from Cartwright an opportunity to present their case for a church in Cartwright to Methodist decision makers. The Methodist district assembly delayed action during the drought years, but finally approved organization of a Cartwright church in 1905.

Those who moved from the Cartwright school Sunday meeting to the new Methodist church may have worried early on how the change would affect their relationships in the neighborhood. It was soon clear there were enough other issues binding neighbors. The Alhambra roadhouse took the lead.[42]

Cartwright's Good Templars complained for months that young boys were getting inside the roadhouse. Finally, the sheriff raided the place and temporarily closed it.

Cartwright's battle with the Alhambra roadhouse paled in comparison with the larger "War on Evil" raging in Phoenix. Some residents said the town was worse than the raucous Colorado mining towns of Leadville and Cripple Creek. The city was wide open—with legal gambling, prostitution and thirty-one saloons open twenty-four hours, seven days a week—when Margaret and Kate first arrived. It wasn't uncommon to see broken-down old miners lying passed out drunk on the courthouse steps. Highwaymen stalked riders on roads leading to outlying towns and farms, even in the Cartwright District. There were sad stories of local drunks beating their wives and leaving some so destitute the women had no alternative but to turn to prostitution.[43]

New settlers fought hard not to be changed by the desert, but to change the desert into an image made to their liking. They tried to replace the dusty streets and loose morals of Phoenix and its surrounding territory with the paved Victorian beauty and evangelistic righteousness of a new progressive West.

Phoenix's war started off with a bang when it closed down the red light district and sent prostitution to areas outside the city limits, like the Alhambra roadhouse. The War on Evil soldiers next turned their attention to gambling. It didn't fall quite as fast. The pace of the War on Evil quickened in 1905 when a noted evangelist announced a "Christian platform" for Phoenix's election, instructing good church-goers to vote only for candidates who promised support for the anti-gambling ordinance. Not long afterward, the Phoenix City Council raised licensing fees for saloons. The effort closed several saloons. Cartwright's Good Templars watched the subsequent increase in business at the roadhouse. After the sheriff's raid, they were determined to get the roadhouse closed permanently. They succeeded in the fall of 1907. Jack Brooks had to find his Kentucky bourbon somewhere else.[44]

Rain and promise of the dam's completion brought the return of prosperity in 1906. Clubs and social groups multiplied across the Valley. A school of music opened. Roman Catholics organized the Catholic Social

Unions parish schools and a Knights of Columbus lodge. Women around the state lobbied on a number of civic causes, not the least their own suffrage. Over the next years, they pushed for women's suffrage tied to statehood, only to be rebuffed in the final hour. They finally got the vote on an initiative measure later in 1912.[45]

New construction and recharged promotion efforts marked recovery. Water made all the difference. Valley farmers finally enjoyed lush crops and profits. Alfalfa bloomed profusely and grains were thick. Growers shipped melons and figs, while the infant citrus industry got its footing. The big news was cattle, with stockmen who had seen so many cattle die now shipping healthy stock. The Water Users' Association's oversight of canals and delivery of water gave farmers enough confidence to announce, "The good times have come to stay." But good times meant higher land prices, shutting Jack and Kate out of purchasing a place of their own. Kate dug deeper.[46]

One escape was baseball. Every club and business sported their own team. African Americans fielded a segregated league as early as 1897. Glendale, Cartwright and Buckeye teams stayed alive in 1904 when most of the West Valley was dust. The Mexican-Athletics announced reorganization in 1907. Professional teams stopped on their way to or from spring training in Southern California, playing before sellout Valley crowds.[47]

A concrete drop on the Grand Canal, n.d. *Courtesy of the Library of Congress, Prints & Photographs Division, HAER ARIZ,7-TEMP,8—2.*

A view of a wooden bridge across the Grand Canal. *Courtesy of the Library of Congress, Prints & Photographs Division, HAER ARIZ, 7-TEMP, 8—5.*

Boston's Bloomer Girls drew an enthusiastic audience when they came to town in 1900 in the dead of summer to play a hastily put together male team. Special trains brought spectators from Mesa and Tempe to Eastlake Park for the afternoon games, before the days of lighted fields. The men gave a good effort, losing a close first game, 11–10. The next day, the Bloomer Girls "shoved the local team out of the little end of the barn," as the newspaper's writer so eloquently put it.[48]

Some of the hottest action around in 1905–06 occurred on a West Valley dirt lot. There the "farmers" took on all comers, every Saturday and Sunday afternoon. Jack and his older children, including six-year-old Ollie, could usually be found on the sidelines on a Saturday, while Kate stayed home with the youngest two, Henry and Victor.[49]

Several West Valley boys realized their dream when backers put together the semiprofessional "Athletics" team in 1907. One of those was third baseman, Carroll Vinson, son of Kate's good friend, Leolia. Kate's girls, especially Ollie, idolized the Cartwright baseball star.[50]

The town lit up when the Athletics won against Mesa in the twelfth inning in April. After that, downtown storeowners closed up on Friday afternoons so employees and customers could cheer on the team at Eastlake Park. Team backers staged big afternoon fairs with bands and Jack Gibson's cowboy contests in conjunction with home games.[51]

Baseball fever was red-hot by late June when Prescott came to town. The Athletics escorted their rivals and three hundred supporters from the depot, fans cheering all the way. It is sad to say, the hoopla was too much for the Athletics. If that wasn't bad enough, the Athletics let the Globe team trounce them on the Fourth of July at home. Winning drew tenuous support from around the Salt River Valley, losing did not. The Athletics were dead by September. Cartwright's hero, Carroll Vinson, was back to playing amateur ball with the Gas Eaters, pitching a few balls on Sunday afternoon to young Ollie Brooks at home in Cartwright.[52]

Ollie was Kate's "tomboy." The pretty girl with her mother's big grey eyes and wistful smile lived out of doors, running and playing ball every chance she got. She already displayed that rare combination of passion and natural ability to play the game well. She was strong and quick, and could both pitch and hit. Encouraged by players like Carroll Vinson, Ollie's raw talent blossomed.

Kate's girls were growing up. Fannie was already fourteen. Shy and quiet, she was Jack's girl. She graduated from the eighth grade in 1909, forcing Jack and Kate to address a number of thorny issues. The closest high school was in downtown Phoenix, over eight miles from Kate and Jack's home. It was impossible for Jack or Kate to chaperone Fannie's daily ride into town while keeping up their other responsibilities. The problem would multiply as the other girls came along. Kate pushed, knowing that Jack was always soft when it came to the girls' welfare, but she never, in a thousand years, expected the response Jack had for her one evening.

"How about Glendale?" he asked. Kate had to be shocked. The town was a dustbowl, killed when the drought forced most of the farmers dependent on the Arizona Canal to move on. Only three small stores stayed in business in town.[53]

What Kate didn't know was that Glendale had been reborn since the Water Users' took over the Arizona Canal. Land prices rose. The population grew to over a thousand. New neighborhoods were developed. Commerce sprang back to life. Nearly four blocks of new businesses joined those three small surviving stores.[54]

Along with Glendale's rebirth was the resurrection of the sugar beet project. Unable to find Glendale farmers willing to gamble on sugar beets, the company turned to farmers in the East Valley. Unfortunately, the factory wasn't finished on time, so beets sat in metal storage sheds

Glendale Avenue in Glendale, Arizona, 1910. *Courtesy of the Glendale Arizona Historical Society.*

a good month during summer's hottest time. The resulting sugar was brown and unusable. The factory shut down days after opening, leaving beet farmers without pay.[55]

The Roosevelt Dam was finally completed in 1911. Four years late and triple the estimated cost, the dam held stored water and rationalized water delivery for the thirsty Valley below. Former president Theodore Roosevelt was there for the dedication. The ceremony was small news. Down in the Valley, farmers were busy plowing and irrigating good crops of alfalfa and wheat, living orderly lives, paying the bills. Few were busting head gates or shooting neighbors over water in the ditch anymore.[56]

The bigger news was the transformation of the West that the Roosevelt Dam in Arizona set in motion. Dams were built across the West, generating electrical power and changing habitat. Floods were controlled and shortages became a thing of the past, for a while. Farmers and their fields got regular water while new land was opened up to scores of new settlers and big corporate growers. John Wesley Powell's vision was achieved, although the great explorer and visionary did not live to see it. Roosevelt Dam was the first—the model for the new West.

All the while, things were moving fast for Arizona. Statehood made Glendale a possibility for Jack and Kate. Much of the land abandoned

A packing shed close to the railroad. Note the palm frond roof, circa 1910. *Courtesy of the Glendale Arizona Historical Society.*

along the Arizona Canal returned to federal ownership. The government was preparing to give the land back to Arizona as a statehood gift in 1912. Wanting the land productive in the meantime, the government put it up for lease until the transfer when Arizona would sell it to pay for schools. Jack could, hopefully, exchange his sweat equity then for a down payment.

Still, Kate had to ask, "Why Glendale?"

"Schools," Jack replied. Glendale was approved for a new high school, set to start up the next fall.[57]

The place he could get had seventy acres about two miles north of town off Grand Avenue. Included were some good outbuildings to fix up and a sturdy two-story house. There was a proper parlor, good-sized kitchen and nice porch, too. The yard was a mess from the years with no water, but a little irrigation water would change that. Most important was the well. The pump was right outside the back door.

Kate wasn't turning down the offer of schools and clean well water. They enrolled Fannie and Rebecca in the temporary high school which met over a store. The other Brooks children, except Leolia, headed for the Glendale Grammar School.[58]

The Roosevelt Dam dedication, March 18, 1911. The dam contained over one-half million acre-feet, half of its capacity. *Courtesy of the Tempe History Museum.*

The house was a proper home. Once it was scrubbed, Kate was off exploring the Woman's Club, a host of card clubs, the Wednesday Embroidery Club and the Methodist church.[59]

Glendale's First Methodist Episcopal Church survived the years of drought. Coming from a lifelong Methodist background, it was natural that Kate would lead her family to join. She soon found out, however, that without "South" tagged at the end, this Methodist was different. Still, Kate had priorities. Differences between churches paled next to the social contacts First Methodist afforded. Kate had Fannie and Rebecca to launch into Glendale society, not to mention her own social position to consider.

Life around Glendale revolved around water, crops, weather, harvests and markets. Sugar beet men were back a third time. After two failures, the company's only hope was to find growers ignorant of the past failures. The "Russians," as they would always be known in Glendale, were Molokan Christians who had recently fled religious persecution and forced military service in Russia. The immigrants were looking for an opportunity to establish a new farming community where they could live and practice their religion without persecution. Glendale's sugar beet men sold a group of 175 adult Russians four hundred acres southwest of Glendale, with the stipulation that they grow sugar beets. The Russians settled down in 1911 and began immediately, planning to live in tents on their land until they could make enough money off their sugar beet crop to build barns and homes. Glendale's school district provided a separate one-room school for Russian children next to the community's church.[60]

Sadly, the whole sugar venture collapsed again. The factory opened for only short stints in 1912 and 1913 before closing for good, leaving the Russians, like local farmers before them, with beets in the fields. Pressed to make a go of it on their new land, they turned to other field crops and dairy and soon succeeded in building homes and barns.

While completion of the dam supported some degree of prosperity in the Valley, it did not ensure water peace. Many farmers, particularly in the West Valley, held on to a them-versus-us mentality, carefully watching the Water Users' Association and taking offense at closed-door meetings. In 1914, these farmers pushed for, and won, an investigation of the Roosevelt Dam Project by the Reclamation Service. The investigation found many irregularities, including a vast number of acres irrigated by owners with more than the 160 acres limit. Still, the Water Users' Association was thriving on the good economy and sale of electric power. Farmers voted in 1917 to take over the dam from the Department of the Interior, agreeing to pay sixty dollars per acre over ten years—five times the original estimate.[61]

The Glendale Methodist Episcopal Church, incorporated 1897. It was one of the few organizations that survived the drought. *Courtesy of the Glendale Arizona Historical Society.*

A reliable water supply did more than bring Glendale's farms back to life. It coursed through ditches into town, irrigating residential yards of trees, grass and gardens, as well as the town park. With plenty of water, people around Glendale went on a green frenzy, planting 1,500 shade trees, over two thousand rose bushes and fifty thousand new fruit trees.[62]

The prosperity that eluded Kate and Jack for so long was finally theirs. They purchased their land and house. Life there was a modern frenzy with Fannie off to nursing school in Phoenix and Marguritte and Rebecca both in high school with clubs and sports teams. The others, except toddler Leolia, were active in grammar school, playing ball and attending parties, socials and every church function that came along. Kate and Jack spun in a whirl of dances, card parties, club meetings, church functions, private parties and dinners. Without automobiles or telephones, the family of nine grabbed meals when they could, coordinated children's schedules, ran a farm, scrubbed mountains of laundry and somehow managed to all walk in to church together on Sunday morning, clean after the Saturday night baths, large Sunday bows in place.[63]

The only way Kate and Jack pulled it all off was to give the children responsibility early. Older children mothered the younger. Girls had scrub boards and hot irons placed in their hands at the age of six or seven, cooked from the time they could stand on a stool to stir. Jack put the boys to work in the fields. All of the children milked and cared for the animals before and after school. It all worked like a well-oiled machine, until the day after Valentine's Day in 1915. Lighting the stove as she'd done for years, Rebecca spilled a small can of coal oil. Flames quickly engulfed her dress, burning her torso and arms. Hearing the screams, Kate and Marguritte rushed to Rebecca and beat the flames out with their own hands and clothing. Kate took the brunt of the flames as she fought madly. The doctor came quickly and dressed the wounds of all three. Rebecca needed round-the-clock care for over a month. Fannie took leave from nursing school to care for Rebecca and Kate. Rebecca was out of danger by late April.[64]

With Rebecca doing better, Kate could finally get back into the swing of things. A big tent revival was set up in a field just north of Glendale. Advertising for the event began weeks in advance. Kate was drawn to revival like Jack was to bourbon.

True to its promises, the event drew well over one thousand attendees every night. Although only April, the atmosphere inside the tent those spring evenings was warm and thick with the dust of two thousand feet trampling

Don Haley with Reverend and Mrs. Northrup on the Apache Trail to Roosevelt Dam, 1917. The road was dusty and not the place for tuberculars like Don. *Courtesy of the author.*

the dirt floor during the hours-long affair. Hand fans waved violently. Kate could hardly sing for the dust.[65]

Across the tent another woman was also having trouble breathing. Minnie Scholl was a member of First Baptist Church. She came every night to help out, though her real motive was more personal. In a short note to her mother in Missouri, Minnie said:[66]

> *I have been helping with the big tent revival every night. Over one thousand most every night, with many professions of faith. I must leave tent as air is too dusty. Don is attending and seems interested.*[67]

Don was Minnie's younger brother. Both he and Minnie came to Arizona seeking a cure for their tuberculosis.

Kate and Minnie Scholl most likely never met. By the time Kate returned from Prescott that summer, Minnie and her husband Burns were headed home to Missouri with their four small children. But the two women's joint attendance at the revival, and links with First Baptist, set in motion a chain of events that would have far-reaching effects—especially for Kate's daughter Ollie.

3

BRAWNY GIRL

The water smelled different, "funny" Joe would say. Nothing like the mighty river water at home in Hannibal, Missouri. The Mississippi was powerful water. It smelled full of life.

After two weeks of nights spent irrigating, Joe had this new water figured out. It smelled like *dust*, like everything else in this burned up Salt River Valley. Joe was so homesick he wanted to drown himself some lonely night in this worthless water, except he didn't think it had enough in it to sink a man.

What made his homesickness worse was he knew it would be a long time before he went home. It was all his family could do to scrape together the funds to send him West. Joe didn't want to come, but he was the only choice after Minnie got sick and couldn't stop coughing. She'd come to the Valley for the dry air cure, but knew it failed her. All she wanted then was to go home to die. She and Burns packed up the children and took off, Minnie in a railway car, Burns and the children by auto. Don, the youngest Haley brother, begged Minnie to take him back home, too, but she was adamant the dry air would work for him, save his life. That's why they sent Joe: to take care of his younger brother, the copper-haired imp, once so full of mischief. Now Don could barely walk across the room. Tears and grief for Minnie were bad for the cough.

Joe had no trouble finding work haying and threshing. Water from the big canals was keeping this new place booming. Farmers told him there was a big dam up in the mountains holding a million acre-feet. Joe took on night work irrigating, sloshing in the dry-smelling Salt River water, making sure it reached the ends of every row before the allotted share of water ran out. A couple of old feed sacks worked for pillows as he lay on ditch banks trying to sleep, but not so deeply that he missed the next water jam. Truth was, he'd rather spend the night napping on a ditch bank than listening to Don's coughs.

As homesick as he was, Joe sensed opportunity in the dry desert air. It wasn't long before older, established farmers, impressed by the grit in the young man, pointed out possibilities. A of couple men went so far as to encourage him. Joe had been thirsty for those good words his whole life. Drinking them in, he threw his lean young body into more work. All the while, he watched and listened, storing up his new knowledge about desert farming.[68]

Don wasn't strong enough to do more than daily household chores. Joe worried all the time. If he wasn't fretting over bills, he fussed about the work he needed to do. Overshadowing it all, he worried about Don's coughing and weakness. Finally, the two brothers got word that their sister had died. Minnie's husband had his mother to help. Joe and Don's folks, Nannie and Willie, would come for Don.

Their arrival was a shot in the arm for Joe. Nannie and Willie took the load of care for Don off of Joe's shoulders, as well as the household chores. In addition, they added modestly to the household income by churning butter to sell. Joe took the butter, as well as extra eggs and a few vegetables from the large garden they planted to market several times a week. On Sundays, Nannie and Willie attended First Baptist in Glendale. Joe didn't have the time, money or energy for church or anything else. Chances are good his path didn't cross during this time with that of his future bride, Ollie Brooks. She was just sixteen and busy out-maneuvering her mother's efforts to mold her, along with her three older sisters, into a young lady who was well respected in Glendale society.[69]

Kate had her hands full with Ollie. The girl had entered high school two years earlier as a freshman with high expectations. Watching her sisters play baseball on the Sugar Queens team, Ollie was anxious to show her talent. Graduating grammar school the previous spring on the honor roll, she was on track to do well academically in high school while taking the pitcher spot on the high school team. Overnight, however, Ollie changed into an unhappy, argumentative underperformer. The crusade to protect young women from the strains of harsh athletics such as baseball was to blame. Jumping on the bandwagon, the Glendale School Board suddenly shuttered the program just as Ollie stepped forward to play. Hurt, disappointed and enraged, Ollie flat-out refused to go back to school after the Christmas break. Why bother?[70]

The Glendale Union High School Sugar Queens basketball team, n.d. *Courtesy of the Glendale Arizona Historical Society.*

There wasn't much for a female high school dropout to do when all her friends were in school. Ever busy, Kate pushed Ollie into the job of Sunday school secretary, dragged her to Missionary Circle and forced Ollie to tag along on social calls. Ollie escaped briefly with a job at the town confectionery. What Ollie wanted was to be outside helping Jack in the fields, but Kate vetoed most of that.[71]

Jack had plenty of work for someone to do. It was a good time to be farming in the Salt River Valley. Europe's eruption into paralyzing, bloody war created huge demand for everything Glendale farmers produced. Arizona's mines buzzed overtime. Salt River Valley farmers responded, planting more and diversifying their crops. The Department of Agriculture noted fifteen different crops with at least five hundred acres in cultivation each in the Salt River Valley. Around Glendale, that included grapes, apricots, plums and cantaloupes. Farm experts said Glendale was one of the areas suitable for citrus and urged farmers and residents to plant all they could.[72]

Valley cotton production rose modestly from its beginnings in 1911 to over 7,000 acres in 1916. The more meaningful figure for local farmers was price. Long staple cotton brought in forty-three cents per pound that season, almost double the 1911 prices. The move to cotton began a significant shift from alfalfa pasturage and spurred the sell-off of dairy cows. A few miles southwest of Glendale, the Goodyear Tire and Rubber Company bought 24,000 acres, rushing 1,500 into production for tires and war-related products.[73]

Jack jumped into cotton, making a good profit. He bought his first automobile, a Model T Ford Speedster. By 1916, almost everyone in town had a vehicle. Rebecca rode into Phoenix with Jack to pick up the new car, since he knew nothing about operating one. Neither did Rebecca, who burned up the brakes on that first trip. Brakes repaired and a little more knowledgeable, Jack piled Marguritte, Ollie and the younger three children into the vehicle for a day's outing in the foothills north of town a couple of weeks later. About a month after that, Marguritte wrecked the car, crushing her foot and laying her up for the rest of the summer. By late August, Jack had the car repaired again and drove the rest of the children up to Prescott for a few days, camping along the way up the winding and steep mountain roads. He, Rebecca, Marguritte and Ollie had gained a lot of automobile knowledge in a short space of time. It was Ollie, though, who always cranked the thing up, cleaned the spark plugs and changed the tires.[74]

Fannie finished her training at Deaconess Hospital and began taking private nursing assignments. Marguritte was a senior at Glendale High. Graduated, Rebecca was home now and pressed into Kate's social life. Rebecca had other ideas. His name was Luther Harris and he worked for Jack. Although Luther was not well educated, he worked at self-educating and wrote poetry.

Luther was not Rebecca's first beau. Earlier in the year, she spent time with Leo Varney, one of six baseball-playing brothers from Missouri. Things didn't work out between Rebecca and Leo, probably because Luther started working in Rebecca's father's fields. Luther and Rebecca married early in 1917 in a small ceremony at Prescott, with Kate as their witness. Fannie would later marry Leo.[75]

President Wilson's neutrality pledge was strained to the breaking point in those early days of 1917. Most people thought the nation was headed for war. Speculation came to an end in March. "No one can doubt any longer. It is to be war," Glendale's newspaper declared. Congress passed the war resolution a week later. Towns across the country, like Glendale, were quickly turned upside down by departing troops and organization for war relief. Hundreds of men converged on Glendale's town hall the day after the war resolution with guns and rifles, ready to protect home and property from any enemy threat. What had been near and familiar was suddenly fearful.[76]

The draft came fast, requiring all men, aged twenty-one through thirty-one, to register. Sign-up was in town on a Saturday in early May. Marguritte Brooks helped out so she could survey all the eligible young bachelors. Joe Haley requested, and received, exemption as a farmer and sole supporter of his family. Not all eligible men showed up, however. The largest group of no-shows was men of Glendale's Molokan Russian community. Their absence wasn't a misunderstanding. It was a matter of principle.[77]

The Molokans were pacifists. They emigrated to their "Promised Land," believing the United States Constitution guaranteed them freedom to practice their religion and pacifist beliefs. Their community had grown to approximately one thousand by the day the United States entered the war.[78]

Eight cars made their way down Lateral 20 west of Glendale not long after the mandatory draft registration deadline. Slowly, the cars turned into the small road that formed the center of the Russian community. It was more than an hour before the cars and their occupants headed north in another cloud of dust.[79]

The visit to the Russians was all the talk around Glendale by afternoon. The Assistant United States Attorney himself came in an attempt to get the Russians to comply with registration requirements. United States law, the assistant attorney explained to Molokan leaders, required even conscientious objectors to register. The Molokans, however, had a long sorry history with government officials in their native Russia. Their leaders told the assistant attorney that their religion forbade even signing their names to anything related to war. The assistant attorney and his entourage left with the situation at an impasse. Farmers talking outside the Flour and Feed said the assistant attorney wouldn't give a regular 100 percent American the second chance he gave the Russians.[80]

"Slacker" was the name quickly and publicly assigned to anyone around Glendale found not giving their "fair share" to the war effort. There were Red Cross slackers, draft slackers, thrift stamp slackers and Liberty Bond slackers, to name just a few. Slackers were publicly derided, their names conspicuously absent from lists of contributors printed on the town newspaper's front page.

People just had to look down the alphabetical listings to see if so-and-so gave. If not, he was a slacker.[81]

The slacker campaign and Glendale's reaction to the Russian's refusal to register exposed an animosity toward minorities that was hardened by mining conflicts around the state. The war in Europe created a big demand for Arizona copper and all workers wanted a larger share of the boom. When they didn't get it, they went out on strike. The strike in Clifton-Morenci shut down the mines during a time when copper sold at the highest prices in eight years. It left a legacy of hate and distrust between peoples that spread far beyond the mining district.[82]

The strike built resentment among Glendale's middle class toward Mexican workers, aliens and anyone else outside the controlling social group. Newspaper coverage was heavy throughout the state, with editors portraying the striking miners as pro-German radicals because of the involvement of the socialist International Workers of the World in the strike. Sentiment in Glendale ran high on the side of mining management because several of Glendale's young men worked in mining mid-management. Once companies shut and locked mines, Glendale's sons came home, bringing their hot talk with them. The strike ended after five months, with workers receiving raises of 5 to 15 percent. During that time, management supporters around the state came to see Mexicans as radical pro-German Wobblies.[83]

This pent-up "patriotism" was just looking for a vehicle for expression. That vehicle arrived in June 1917, when, as Glendale's Russians argued their case in Phoenix, copper workers in the southern Arizona town of Bisbee went on strike over unequal pay and treatment of foreign and minority workers. This time, however, the local citizenry, in the name of pro-war patriotism, wasted no time. On July 12, two thousand vigilantes rounded up almost 1,200 men, many of them Mexicans, and loaded them into boxcars that the vigilantes then deposited outside of the state of Arizona. The train eventually ended up in Hermanas, New Mexico, where it sat for two days in the summer sun until federal troops arrived. Two men died. The deportees remained in New Mexico under federal protection for another two months. All subsequent suits against the vigilantes and mining companies were dismissed.

The threat of slacker humiliation motivated Joe Haley to buy into the war effort. His name appeared in the newspaper for the first time since he moved to Glendale two years before, when he succumbed to unavoidable pressure to buy one dollar's worth of Liberty Bonds in June 1917. The "investment" kept the wolves away and put Joe in the "Loyal Citizen" column for a while. Good citizen or slacker: there was no middle ground.[84]

Thirty-five draft-age Molokan men stood before the United States marshal in Phoenix a month after the dusty visit by the assistant United States attorney. Outside the courthouse, members of the Molokan community demonstrated, women reportedly wailing and throwing themselves to the ground. Inside, the marshal sentenced all thirty-five men to a year in the Yavapai County jail in Prescott. They did not go peacefully. Wives and mothers demonstrated outside the Glendale depot and along the train route to Prescott. Twenty-eight Russians were arrested for inciting a riot. A large contingent of vacationers from Glendale met the train in Prescott to get a look at the prisoners. The war hadn't slowed the annual summer exodus out of the Valley. Glendale's newspaper carried news of the vacationers in Prescott spotting the Russians on work detail around the mountain town for the rest of the summer.[85]

Joe Haley continued as he had, working day and night, pinching every cent that came his way. It all finally paid off in October when he succeeded in purchasing a twenty-acre farm three miles west of Glendale, on the west side of the Russian community. Joe put $2,000 down, agreeing to a total selling price of $5,250. His first payment of $250 came due the following January, with $500 due the same time the next year. Only then would the former owners write a mortgage for the remainder, payable by 1923 at 7 percent interest.[86]

What Joe got in return was a two-room wooden house, a few outbuildings and some of the best agricultural soil in the world. The house resembled a tuberculosis tent house with its screened openings on the south and north sides that could be covered during cold or rain with heavy canvas awnings that were rolled up on the outside of the house. The awnings were almost worthless during the annual summer dust storms. An open breezeway running north and south separated the kitchen/living area from the small second room, used as a sleeping room until it was too hot. Beds were moved into the yard then. Two ditches between the house and the road to the east fed the farm. One was the Water Users' lateral, delivering water from the Arizona Canal, five miles to the north. The other carried the water from the lateral to Joe's land. Trees, planted by the original homesteaders some twenty years earlier, shaded the house and buildings. Two ash and four cottonwoods lined the ditch, forming a canopy over the narrow roadway of Lateral 21 and shielding the house on the east side. A chinaberry shaded the door and part of the roof from the harsh northwest summer afternoon sun. Three ash trees shaded the small yard south of the house, another one the wash lawn on the north. Four more lined the drive to the south. Native screw bean mesquites marked the northern boundary of Joe's land. A small orchard of plum, pear, peach and apricot trees stood just the other side of the wash line. Blackberries and grapevines clung to the fence. Barbed wire fencing, strung tightly between mesquite poles, defined the property, separating fields planted with alfalfa. Trees used to shade houses on desert farms were a combination of nostalgia and survival before any form of air conditioning. Grass, rose bushes and the like were the miracle of irrigation.

Joe faced a river of his own sweat to make those initial mortgage payments, even in good times. Added to them, he had his Water Users' assessments to pay, as well as a team of horses, farming equipment, seed and a couple of milk cows to buy and a pump house to build over the twenty-foot well. He continued to hire himself out for cash to pay for it all, working his own place in his "spare" time.

He spent a bit of that time each week talking with farmers gathered at the Flour and Feed. There, Joe caught up on prices, as well as the vital news about what farmer might need a little extra help. He took a fair share of ribbing about his neighbors, those Russians living just across the road. They didn't bother Joe, except when one of their sheep escaped and came wandering down the road. Nannie, Willie and Don Haley often reported watching the Russian wagons, or sometimes a funeral procession, headed for the little Russian church.[87]

The war dug deeper into everyone's lives around Glendale. Civic clubs and lodges fell over each other in the stampede to take leadership of the town's home front efforts. The Woman's Club plunged 100 percent into the Red Cross effort, from fund raising to knitting socks. Kate Brooks was at the head of the pack, making the first Red Cross honor roll for her fund raising efforts. The Odd Fellows, with Jack installed as Noble Grand, set up support networks for the families of members serving in the armed forces.

War mobilization stepped up demand for wheat, beef, citrus and milk. Glendale farmers and housewives scrambled to deliver. Federal Food Administration director Herbert Hoover's message to "Save the Waste and Win the War" played powerfully in frugal Glendale. Officials advised that fruit growing operations, large and small, dry every peach and plum. By winter, Glendale was on Hoover's bandwagon of "wheatless" Mondays and Wednesdays and "porkless" Tuesdays and Saturdays. Officials urged housekeepers to cook with lamb and corn meal so that soldiers could have the more popular beef and wheat. Valley farmers tried to take advantage of the demand amidst an environment of federal price controls. A new milk condensing plant in the Valley begged for all the milk local dairies could produce, only to discover that Valley farmers had sold off their herds to grow cotton. The trend toward long staple cotton rushed forward. Arizona cotton farmers planted 35,400 acres in 1917, quadruple the acreage of 1916, reaping almost $365 an acre, an increase of $150 over the prior year for high grade cotton.[88]

Returning to the Valley in September, Glendale's citizens focused all club and civic activity on the war effort. With club agendas cancelled, social life hinged on the private. Kate visited a week with friends in the Cartwright District, hosted dinner parties and a big Thanksgiving dinner, and was guest at several similar functions throughout the fall. Ollie escaped Kate's social whirl by spending as much time as she could at newlywed Rebecca's home, south of Glendale. Fannie politely advertised her availability for private nursing assignments. Her first was helping after the birth of Rebecca's first child, Alden. Kate and Jack were now grandparents.[89]

Leaders at First Baptist thought the lull in Glendale's social scene was the perfect time for revival. Unlike the big tent crusade of two and one-half years before, this was to be a 100 percent *Baptist* revival. Even that distinction, it turned out, didn't define things tightly enough for some.

An outspoken lay leader with strong Texas Southern Baptist connections secured the revival speaker. The revivalist, Mississippi evangelist T.T. Martin, was a strict Southern fundamentalist on a crusade to return the churches to what he termed "New Testament" purity. Martin was a particularly forceful speaker bent on exposing to lay members of Northern Baptist churches the evils of modernism and the eternal pitfalls of doctrinal controversies growing in intensity among Northern Baptist clergy. Later, in the early 1920s, Martin would change his focus, authoring the popular, *Hell in the High Schools*, warning parents and school officials of the dangers of teaching evolution, and joining William Jennings Bryan on the crusade leading to the Scopes Trial. Helping Martin with the First Baptist revival was a West Texas singing leader by the name of Woodie Smith.[90]

Martin left confusion in his wake. After his departure, rumor got out that Martin's preaching convicted First Baptist's own Reverend Northrup that he was never properly baptized by full immersion by an ordained Baptist minister. As a result, rumor claimed Reverend Northrup was secretly re-baptized by Smith after Martin left town. Reverend Northrup denied the allegations but seems to have been either unable or unwilling to get the West Texas singing leader, Woodie Smith, to move on and let the church calm down. Smith, instead, hung around for another week in an attempt to secure the rebaptisms of members not properly baptized according to the strict view presented by Martin. Only three actually went back under the water, but just about everyone in the church was churned up. More than a few began questioning their church and pastor that fall of 1917.[91]

Late in May, a delegation of Glendale businessmen drove out to the Russian colony to find out firsthand why Russians did not purchase bonds. Before the meeting was over, some did. Their young men came home from jail a few days later, having served only ten months. When the Russian crowd began to assemble to welcome the train at the Glendale depot, local officials told Russian leaders to make the homecoming quiet and to disperse the crowd fast.[92]

The summer of 1918 came and went much like all the others in Glendale, war or no war. Early in the summer, Kate drove her Sunday school class to a picnic at the river. She and Fannie spent several weeks on the California coast so that Fannie could recover from recent throat surgery. At home, Marguritte and Ollie kicked up their heels a little while Kate was gone. Young matron Rebecca joined her sisters and some of their friends for a day of fun and swimming at a nearby public swimming pool, all of them posing for pictures, daringly dressed in men's sailor suits. As summer ended, Ollie optimistically returned to high school.[93]

No one had cornered the market on optimism that fall. News reports said the boys still alive would be home soon. Before anyone could get too comfortable, a new terror descended. Spanish Influenza hit the nation, killing 4,500 in Philadelphia and 3,200 in Chicago during just one week in October. The numbers were impossible to fathom until the flu hit locally. By the time it was over, ten times more Americans died from the flu that year than by German bombs or bullets during the entirety of the war.[94]

The epidemic spread like wildfire. Public officials grappled with questions of the nature of the disease and their own powers to control cities, schools and businesses. The State Superintendent of Public Health issued a warning on September 29 for people to refrain from spitting, kissing and drinking from common cups. The epidemic rolled right over the warning. By October 10, Phoenix, a city of approximately twenty-eight thousand, had one hundred cases of influenza; five days later, fifteen people were dead. The County Medical Society recommended that officials close all schools, churches, theatres and other meeting places. Businesses dependent upon open public meetings saw their livelihoods go down the drain.[95]

Fannie Brooks caught the flu in the early days of the epidemic as she nursed sufferers at Deaconess Hospital. Like all of Kate's children, Fannie had a strong constitution and pulled through quickly. Recovered, she began a full schedule of private nursing in Glendale as whole families fell ill and could not care for one another. With the mandatory closing of churches, newspapers printed the weekly sermons of local pastors along with reminders for parishioners to send their tithes and offerings in so churches could pay their bills.

Thirty-five died in Glendale during the first three weeks of November. The hardest hit were Mexican nationals living in crowded conditions, particularly in cotton camps. Glendale converted the high school building into an emergency hospital just as Phoenix converted its Woman's Club building for the same purpose. Many volunteers risked their own lives.[96]

The influenza was especially hard on the very young, the old and the weak. Don Haley took sick in late November and died in early December. Willie, Nannie and Joe buried him in the Glendale cemetery, with Reverend Northrup officiating. Nannie sadly wrote "Our Darling Boy died Dec. 8th, 1918" in the family Bible, right under similar statements for Minnie and the other two children Nannie and Willie lost as toddlers.

It looked like the epidemic was over by mid-December in the Valley. Theatre owners pressed hard for officials to lift the restrictions. Church services resumed on December 13, but Glendale schools remained closed until after Christmas. Critics warned that the germs were still around and that the Valley could be hit a second time, but people hoped the cynicism was wrong for a sunny "health center" like the Valley. Sadly, the cynics won the bet. Glendale schools, closed for forty-eight days, opened for just two before newspapers reported over two hundred new influenza cases. Glendale school officials, already facing the threat of having to hold all students back a year, opted to close only grades one through seven. County health officials overrode Glendale's decision and closed the schools down immediately. The epidemic played out more quickly the second time around and schools opened again on January 24, this time without Ollie Brooks. A week later, school officials announced they would not hold students back but would, instead, cut all nonessentials, like Spanish and music, lengthen school days and add Saturday classes in order to pass students along on time.[97]

The epidemic left families mourning across the nation. Joe took Don's death hard. If Willie and Nannie thought about going home to Missouri after burying Don, one look at Joe changed their minds. He was breaking himself on that little farm, throwing all he had into the dream he never let himself have all those years ago back in Missouri. With the war and epidemic over, Joe saw a glimmer of light in his dream. That light was cotton.

A lot had happened since those gambling Valley farmers planted a few hundred acres of cotton back in 1911. The boom in auto tire sales, coupled with war demands for airplane tires and parachutes, created a huge demand for cotton just when shipping disruptions caused by the war cut off supplies from Egypt. The proximity of the Goodyear Tire and Rubber Plant drove Valley farmers to plant the new, high-quality long staple cotton, netting higher yields and even better market prices. Farmers like Joe across the Valley were drunk on the prospect of what cotton could do for them. He had only twenty acres, but it didn't take long for Joe to decide to put the majority of it in cotton. It was the right decision. That first crop of cotton enabled him to pay his first installment of $250 on the farm early.[98]

Cotton euphoria took many forms. Glendale's Commercial Club made cotton their top priority and sponsored a mass meeting for farmers to meet with the state entomologist to get information on how to protect crops from pests. The French delegate to the World Cotton Conference, on a tour of the Valley's reclamation project and cotton fields, said Salt River Valley cotton was better than Egyptian and urged Valley farmers to plant more. Local farmers didn't need much convincing. Salt River Valley cotton commanded the highest prices in the world. Glendale cotton production rose 400 percent. Other crops saw significant gains, too. Lettuce production rose from 10 to 81 carloads a year later, district cantaloupe shipments increased from 366 carloads to 552. It was a banner year for peaches and apricots. All of it depended on an expansion of water resources.[99]

The good economy extended beyond farms. Glendale's population approached two thousand, with hundreds more living in the surrounding district. Glendale schools bulged. Grammar school attendance rose 55 percent in one year. High school attendance more than doubled, prompting the school board to talk of building a second. All those residents and children meant more business in town. Mercantile businesses and commercial construction doubled.

Joe rode the cotton wave and paid his $500 payment, due January 1, 1920, early, securing his mortgage. Salt River Valley farmers planted 186,000 acres of cotton in the spring of 1920, transferring over 40,000 acres in alfalfa, 10,000 in pasturage and 2,000 in cantaloupes from the year before.[100]

A few black clouds peeked around the Salt River Valley that glowing spring, but optimism ran so high not many paid any attention. Farmers were busy selling off the last of their dairy herds and manure, luxuriating in new freedoms now that they weren't tied to milking twice a day. The Valley had already lost over half of its 55,000 head of dairy cows in just the two years between 1917 and 1919. Eight local cheese factories and the brand new condensed milk cannery closed because they couldn't get the milk. It wasn't only dairy farmers converting to cotton. Wheat production fell dramatically.

Bankers and chamber of commerce men became alarmed with this trend and tried to scare farmers by predicting that concentration on a single crop spelled disaster, but Valley farmers didn't trust the advice of bankers or businessmen whose hands stayed clean all day.[101]

The pressing problem from farmers' perspective was labor supply. The postwar boom only served to make things more cutthroat. Chronic labor shortages created a competitive and sometimes raucous agricultural labor market in which some farmers thought nothing of offering their neighbor's workers a few cents more to walk off the neighbor's fields and right onto theirs. At a market potential of a dollar and a quarter a pound for cotton, the stakes got so high for local cotton growers that many banded together through the Arizona Cotton Growers' Association to control the wage scale and increase the labor supply by importing whole families from neighboring Mexico to pick the 1920 bumper cotton crop. Valley farmers complained they were forced to pay the highest price in the world for labor and equipment to produce the 1920 cotton crop.[102]

Cotton was barely picked and ginned that fall when the bottom fell out of the market. Many Valley farmers later said that the Cotton Crash of 1920 was much worse than even the Great Depression. The sudden drop took most local farmers by complete surprise when they first heard in mid-September they couldn't sell their crop. Scrambling to understand why, local cotton growers heard first that the shutdown was a result of a virtual halt in the textile and tire industries. The immediate advice for farmers was to hold. The Arizona Cotton Growers' Association secured short term funding and storage in an attempt to tide their members over until the market picked up. Farmers soon realized it would take longer than a few months for the market to absorb both the 5 million pounds of stored cotton released by the government as well as the many tons Egypt dumped on European buyers. Cotton farming was only one part of a widespread postwar recession that lasted three years, bankrupting over half a million farmers.[103]

Joe couldn't afford a season with a loss. His solution was to get out of cotton quick, but the cotton slump soon spread to other crops, drying up markets for Valley cattle and cantaloupes. Banks and the chambers of commerce urged farmers to get back into dairy, but no one had the hefty dollars it took to repurchase herds and buy new equipment. Under intense pressure from members, the Water Users' Association halted all development work and extended water for a brief time to farmers unable to pay; but with 65 percent of their members in that category, Water Users' president, F.A. Reid, bluntly said the association couldn't give out free water for long. Those in arrears would be assessed.[104]

His dream crumbling around him, Joe Haley began playing a game of evasion. He bought time on his 1921 mortgage payment by paying the interest and quitclaim deeding the land over to Nannie. Even making the interest payment took every cent he had, leaving nothing for seed, water or a meager living until he could plant and harvest a crop of some kind. The lines of Joe's face grew deeper. He looked fifty instead of thirty-one. Help came from an unexpected source. A longtime Glendale farmer Joe had worked for off and on offered to loan him enough money to tide him over. Joe was shocked and humbled by the offer. Immediate crisis averted and a good crop of alfalfa in the field, Nannie decided it was time for more change.

Over the years, Joe always put his own spin on the story of what happened next. He held court one summer afternoon years later on a lush lawn sloping down to the mighty Mississippi. Big dinner finished, the young bucks of the family didn't have to try very hard to goad "Uncle Joe" into retelling what had become known as his "Brawny Girl" story. Joe was always eager to oblige.

> *I'd been in the Salt River Valley four years and was already one of the most successful young farmers around when I decided it was time to take a wife. It was 1921. I had a nice place out in Arizona, one any woman around would be proud to call home.*

Joe paused, studying his calloused, worn hands before him. The nails that weren't smashed and permanently black were neat and clean on Sunday. He wore his one dress shirt open at the throat now that church was over; his dark dress pants; and good black shoes, which were shined by Ollie every Saturday. Joe took a deep breath and continued.

> *Saturday was the big town day back then. Farmers would come to Glendale to do their tradin'. Wives and family came, too, to shop and socialize a bit. Town buzzed. I know if I am going to find the right woman, my best bet will be on a Saturday.*
>
> *I clean myself up real early and go on in to town on several consecutive Saturdays. Look good, if I do say so myself, he chuckled. Each week I park myself nonchalantly on a key spot, you see, so I can watch the traffic come into town.*

Ollie couldn't stand to hear the story again. Anger rising in her throat, she pushed back from the big table there on the lawn of Joe's cousin on the banks of the Big River. Letting herself into the kitchen through the back door, she poured a glass of cool too-sweet tea. Closing her eyes, she took a deep breath.

She could see all the young people sitting around Joe, faces turned toward him in adoration.

"Damn!" she thought. "He'll be impossible to live with the rest of this damn trip."

> *Now, one Saturday along down the road comes this buckboard wagon with two girls in it. One girl is petite and all frilly. The buckboard stops in front of the candy store there on the avenue and the frilly girl gets down and goes on in. Nice to look at, I think to myself, but forget her. Then the buckboard goes on down the street to the Flour and Feed. That girl driving the wagon is the complete opposite of the frilly girl. This second, brawny girl proceeds to tie up the horse and wagon and go on inside the store. Pretty soon, out the brawny girl comes, hauling a hundred-pound sack of feed like it was nothing.*
>
> *I know right then I'd found my girl: a brawny girl. I track her down to First Baptist Church and make my appearance. The rest, as they say, is history.*

The roar told Ollie that Joe had delivered his punch line. Thinking it safe to return, she stepped onto the back step.

"But Uncle Joe," a favorite nephew interrupted, "I thought you met Aunt Ollie when your Ford broke down in front of the Water Users' office in town and you couldn't get it cranked up. Aunt Ollie came along and asked if she could help crank the automobile. You're thinking 'this is some joke,' when the smaller sister tells you the brawny girl is the official 'cranker' in their family. 'She even cranks it up for our paw,' the sister said."

Joe leaned back, a laugh on his face. "So, you say, 'Go ahead and give it a try,'" the nephew continued.

"You knew you'd found a wife when that brawny girl cranked up that old Ford like it was nothing," the younger man concluded as everyone laughed, eyes expectantly on Joe as Ollie slid back into her chair.

"Well, it might have happened that way," Joe replied, those big ears of his turning red.

"Which way was it, Aunt Ollie?" someone asked.

"You wouldn't believe it if I told you," Ollie replied as she picked up a large platter and began to clear the table. Joe's sister Maggie and a couple of the other women shook their heads as they, too, gathered up dishes. They knew the truth about the "Brawny Girl" stories, and a whole lot more.

Ollie Brooks, circa 1919. *Courtesy of the author*.

4

HUNTING FOR NORMAL

The application of water is approaching a science," declared the visiting government statistician who had come to survey irrigation works in the summer of 1920.[105]

Salt River Valley farmers didn't need some government man to tell them what they already knew. They were avid scientific agriculturalists. Just the year before, West Valley farmers packed the Woman's Club in Glendale to hear the county agent tell them how best to irrigate their cotton. They went out and practiced the method, producing a cotton bounty sure to make them all rich. What Valley farmers didn't count on was the one thing they could not control. Cotton was a commodity, buffeted about by international politics. With the war over and the embargoes lifted, Egypt dumped its stores and the United States released its surplus, flooding the market and leaving American farmers holding the bag.[106]

Nannie watched her son struggle through those lessons, almost losing everything he'd worked night and day for over the last four years. It wasn't much—only twenty acres and a poor house—but it was all he had. She and Willie helped, but Nannie knew Joe needed someone to work the fields and milk the cows, so he could rent himself out for cash. Nannie knew, too, he needed another side of life besides work. Joe needed a wife.

It was only after Don's death that Nannie found time to attend Women's Missionary Circle at First Baptist in Glendale. She must have raised a few eyebrows the first time she walked into that room full of corsets and lace. After all she'd been through, Nannie cared little for fashion. She was a wren of a woman in old fashioned mourning, her long thin breasts hanging loose until they rested on the sizable round of her stomach. She gathered her stringy yellow-gray hair functionally at the back of her neck. A pair of glasses perched on her definite nose. As much as Kate Brooks dressed to fit in, Nannie Haley was dressed to stay out.[107]

There weren't many young women at First Baptist Nannie would consider capable or willing to take on the job of marrying her son. It wouldn't be easy. Joe's wife would face a complex web of relationships and bonds. Nannie singled Ollie Brooks out and spent months getting to know the shy girl. Nannie was sure she and Ollie would enjoy each other's company on a day-to-day basis. A marriage between Joe and Ollie was more questionable. The girl was stubborn to a fault, but Nannie saw that as a positive character trait in this case. It would take that and more to stand up to Joe's temper.

Nannie was a good judge. Any other young woman would have run in the opposite direction. Ollie looked at it differently. She was all but locked indoors cooking, cleaning and throwing parties while Kate conducted one of the most ambitious social careers in Glendale. An opportunity to break free, work outside and be treated kindly by Nannie Haley sounded like heaven to Ollie, in contrast. Past the run-down house and backbreaking labor, Ollie saw the promise of kindness and freedom. Nannie and Willie drew Ollie like a magnet. She didn't know Joe, except from a few buggy rides after Sunday dinners. She hoped he turned out to be like her sister Rebecca's husband, Luther.

That no one prepared Ollie for her marriage night was clear years later on the eve of her own daughter, Genevieve's, wedding. Prompted by a sister-in-law, Ollie attempted to bring up the subject of "a man and a woman" to Genevieve one morning while she ate breakfast. Her hands in soapy water, back to her daughter, Ollie finally withdrew in frustration and embarrassment, saying "Oh, I can't do this," as she stomped out the back door.[108]

Joe and Ollie married early one January afternoon in 1922 in Reverend Northrup's parlor with just their parents in attendance. The bride wore a new homemade dress. Kate hosted a small supper after the ceremony. Rebecca and Luther most likely drove in from their farm three miles south of town. Their three-year-old son, Alden, was a charmer who held the hearts of everyone in the family, especially Ollie. She'd spent as much time as she could at Rebecca and Luther's since the boy's birth.[109]

Marguritte and Fannie missed the wedding dinner. Marguritte was 150 miles away, teaching the children of cattle ranchers in a one-room schoolhouse, high in the mountains of the Mogollon Rim northeast of the Valley. Fannie lived relatively close, but kept to herself since her marriage to Leo Varney in the spring of 1920. Henry, Victor and Leolia still lived at home and, thus, couldn't escape cleanup duty.[110]

The transition to her new life was something of a surprise to Ollie, given her eagerness to get out from under Kate's thumb. Years later, Ollie told a friend she was so homesick during those early days living on the farm that she thought she was going to die. She might as well have moved to another country, life was so different.

The sickness Ollie felt was more than emotions. Waves of nausea crashed suddenly, weakening the usually strong, healthy Ollie.

"Oh, Honey," Nannie tried to soothe. "It's the stork telling you he's coming."[111]

Stunned, Ollie sat glued to her chair as Nannie bustled about the kitchen to brew her special tea for this ailment. Ollie wanted her own children, but not so soon. Nannie comforted Ollie through the early weeks of marriage and morning sickness. It was what Nannie did best, naturally. Nannie made the young woman feel special. Years later, she would say, "Nannie was my best friend."

The security Nannie provided allowed Ollie to see that she was freer on that little farm than she ever was before. It didn't take long to realize that, hidden in the strangeness and isolation of her new surroundings, she could be herself. No more corsets, teas or indoor living. Ollie bobbed her hair, picked up her plow and began to sweat.

There was still Joe. His temper was terrible. Let a piece of equipment break or a neighbor fail to pass on the water in the ditch on time and Joe would explode. Only Nannie could deal with him in those instances. It wasn't long before Ollie committed her own misdeeds, inciting his storm. But there was a line. Nannie's boys would never think of striking a woman.[112]

A counterbalance to Joe's anxiety was the morning breakfast meeting. After milking, Joe and Ollie came in to the breakfast Nannie prepared. Around the big oak table, the four partners read the Bible and prayed before discussing the day's work. Joe often expressed his stress over the workload, bills, small glitches and broken machinery. The other three worked to diffuse his frustration and take some of the load. Everyone left the table knowing what had to be done that morning and who would do it. With the agricultural economy still poor, they weren't out of the woods by a long shot.[113]

No matter how tight the finances, they always managed to pay for delivery of both morning and afternoon papers. It paid off when one of the four saw a small notice from the local Flour and Feed, which was looking for a supplier for five tons of hay. Joe was waiting for the company's doors to open the next morning, jumping on the chance to sell the hay he and Ollie had just cut. The profit allowed them to pay on the mortgage loans and add to the small herd of registered Holsteins. He and Ollie figured they could handle the extra work of milking. Nannie and Ollie would churn the cream into butter that Joe took to market daily to be shipped, on ice, to the big markets in Los Angeles. Joe added Ollie's name to the next quitclaim as they caught up on the mortgage payments.[114]

The crash of 1920–21 marked the end of an era for farmers. American farmers had responded to urgent needs of the war with improved efficiency, machinery and production. The emergency over, supply outstripped demand, especially in the face of renewed foreign competition. For the next twelve years, *farmers* were the problem. Farmer purchasing power steadily deteriorated. Not of one voice, farmers looked for solutions from price and production controls to tariffs.[115]

Glendale's farmers lived the "farm problem." Some—like lettuce, melon and poultry farmers—pushed into new markets by improved icing, found times exciting. For others, they were times for despair.[116]

Bankers warned before the crash against monocrop farming, but with little impact. Dairymen, wanting out of the drudgery and small profits, sold off cows by the thousands. Hats in hands after the cotton crash, farmers returned to banks for loans to buy back cows and equipment. Merchants, needing customers, got behind the move. Armour initiated a program to bring in cows. The Water Users' supported farmers with a one-dollar-an-acre refund on assessments, backed by the United States government.[117]

Hard times made Valley farmers testy. Some never got the "protective association" fever of old canal war days out of their system. The target was Water Users' and its decision to add forty thousand acres in Buckeye and five thousand in Queen Creek, drawing down the water table, many farmers said. Farmers wanted efficiency, accountability and, most of all, a voice. Aside from expanding, Water Users' embarked on alleviating the serious water logging and alkali build-up brought on by surface water irrigation on over eighty thousand acres. Pumping needed electricity, spurring the association to build two additional dams, followed by construction of a dam to supply power for copper-mining operations. Built principally for power, these three dams added another 370,000 acre-feet of capacity and brought irrigation water to an additional ten thousand acres. In addition, the Association said it would reclaim 70,000 acre-feet through its canal concreting efforts.[118]

As Arizona farmers debated dams and pumping, the focus was shifting to a new playing field, one that would occupy the imagination of much of the Southwest for the next half-century. Responding to the demands of a new age, those interested in western reclamation began to talk about more than flood control and irrigation. Attention turned now to harnessing the "big" river, the Colorado, with a high dam to generate power for the cities. Driving the charge was growth in Los Angeles and agricultural development in Imperial Valley in the far southeastern corner of the state.

Developers of Imperial Valley eyed the river as early as 1849, when they tried to bring some of its water inland for irrigation through the fertile delta land of Mexico. Problems with part of the delivery canal running through Mexico drove farmers and developers to push for an all-American canal that would drain from the Colorado further north. California's canal plan was eclipsed in the early 1910s, however, by a plan between the state, Los Angeles and the federal government to build the world's highest dam at a site just south of the Nevada line. The plan raised more than a few red flags in the other six states bordering the Colorado River (Arizona, Nevada, Utah, New Mexico, Colorado and Wyoming), setting in motion a multi-year process to hammer out a treaty covering water allocation, power ownership and construction of the dam.

Apportionment was a loaded gun in the West, where prior-use rights gave California the advantage and appeared to be supported by a recent Supreme Court ruling. At the heart of the debate were key questions of states' versus federal rights, regarding everything from ownership of streambeds to the power generated by the proposed dam to states, like Arizona, that stood to lose tax revenue if the federal government claimed ownership of the power generated by the dam. Private power companies, including the Salt River Valley Water Users' Association, lobbied heavily behind states' rights advocates because to do otherwise could mean the federal government owned the power generated by the new dam, undermining private power companies' position.

Representatives of the seven states met in Santa Fe in 1922 to pound out a final agreement with Herbert Hoover presiding. The principal goal was allocation between the Upper Basin (Wyoming, Utah, Colorado and New Mexico) and Lower Basin (Nevada, Arizona and California). Californians were disappointed in not receiving resolution on water storage and hydroelectricity. Still, all of the representatives, including Arizona's, signed the Colorado River Compact to be ratified by Congress and the legislatures of the seven states.

In the meantime, George W.P. Hunt took office as Governor of Arizona for the fourth time, defeating the incumbent and supporter of the compact, Thomas Campbell. With the mines and Water Users' behind him, Hunt blocked ratification, insisting that Arizona's Gila River not be counted against the state's allocation from the Colorado. The key to Hunt's opposition was his "gut" instinct that the compact and plans for a dam on the Colorado were the work of powerful interests in California who stood to benefit. Hoover thought Hunt a "blunderbuss." Contributing to this impression was the fact Hunt supported the "outlandish" idea of a "high line" canal carrying water from the Colorado River to central Arizona. Hunt stymied Hoover's agenda for the moment, making the compact the center of his for the next four years.[119]

As Governor Hunt focused on the Colorado River Compact, the local economy continued its downward spiral. Failure of the cattle market the spring before was too much for the Glendale State Bank. Trouble cut across sectors. The Phoenix Trades Council handed out free meals to the hungry as local laborers went without work.[120]

Perhaps diversions do best in hard times. Just mention the "game," and men, children and women dropped their troubles for a while and talked like the baseball experts they believed themselves to be. Crowds gathered around the town pharmacy or newspaper office for the early news on the World Series scores in those last years before almost everyone had their own radios.

Local baseball wasn't as flashy, but it had heart and provided plenty of entertainment. Just before the crash in the summer of 1920, Valley baseball supporters organized the Central Arizona League and Glendale gave birth to the Greys.

The Greys were fantastic right out of the gate, winning seven straight games that first summer and creating hysteria almost attractive enough to bring the heat escapees back to town early. Many local Mexican American players were as good or better than Anglo players, but were not usually welcome on teams like the Greys until the teams were in championship races and desperate enough to drop the boundaries. Mexican American players organized their own teams, naming them the Browns and Tigers. African Americans organized the Western Giants and frequently beat the socks off their Anglo or Mexican American opponents. Families packed blankets and a picnic and watched their team play for a Sunday treat.[121]

Merchants attempted to lure customers by declaring a rollback to prewar, "normal" prices, but precious little was "normal." Economic recession was only one of a host of wrenching crises of those early postwar years. The official end of war raised both new and old enemies at home. Chaos and starvation in Eastern Europe brought masses of immigrants to the United States as the Bolshevik Revolution drummed up Americans' fear of foreigners. It was a shock, nonetheless, when Glendale residents opened their local newspaper to read the scathing headline, "People of Glendale: Do you know that people in this town are starving to death?" The allegation pitted Glendale citizens against neighbors and friends, exposing a widening gap in their views on civic responsibility, values and morality.[122]

The problem was the Mexican national families the Arizona Cotton Growers' Association brought up from Mexico to pick the thousands of acres of cotton the summer before the bust. Cash strapped, with their cotton sitting unsold, Association members reneged on their deal. That left an estimated ten thousand pickers in the Salt River Valley, many around Glendale, to fend for themselves. Teachers and school officials alerted the newspaper. By then, the magnitude of the problem was so shocking, the mayor called an emergency mass meeting. The first priority, all agreed, was to feed the destitute. After that, "Get them out of Glendale" fast.[123]

Glendale quickly organized a relief committee, composed of representatives of the town's churches, to evaluate the requests for aid and distribute any relief monies raised. Given the end goal of moving the problem out of Glendale as soon as possible, the committee spent as much time fighting with the Arizona Cotton Growers' Association as they did setting up the temporary process to feed the hungry. Relief officials across the Valley were vocal in their belief that the problem stemmed from the Cotton Growers' Association's failure to fulfill their end of the bargain to return pickers to Mexico. Association spokesmen responded that pickers did not want to go back to certain starvation and unemployment. Cotton growers and pickers alike hoped for a quick market turnaround so pickers could get back in the fields for the next season. To this, Glendale's temporary relief agency spokesmen replied, "Then take care of them while you are waiting to use them."[124]

The Cotton Growers' Association solved the problem by moving several truckloads of pickers away from the racket in Glendale. In the end, the Mexican government paid to return thousands of stranded Mexican nationals back to Mexico, but many others stayed in the Valley, taking whatever agricultural jobs came along. Those who remained in Glendale created a demographic shift in the town, filling schools and creating ongoing needs for relief, especially between crop seasons. Glendale's relief committee made its efforts permanent, establishing the Glendale Welfare Association.

First Baptist opted out of the relief effort because it had its own mission for Glendale's Mexican national community, led by two full-time female missionaries paid for by the church's Men's Missionary Society. First Baptist's focus was principally evangelism and Americanization, not welfare. Reverend Northrup and the missionaries often traveled to fields and camps to hold impromptu services for field workers. A number of converts joined First Baptist before the church organized a separate Spanish-speaking Baptist Church. The mission provided a convenient excuse to stay out of the relief effort, but it was only part of the reason First Baptist chose not to participate. The unity between churches experienced during the war was wearing thin, conservative "fundamentalist" churches huddling together against "modernists."[125]

Glendale's fundamentalist churches began the decade with a revival by a Billy Sunday–sponsored organization. Kate was in charge of organizing support from all of the town's women's organizations. The success of her efforts is unrecorded. The next spring, the group of conservative churches launched a campaign to close all businesses in town on Sunday. Responding to pressure from merchants, theatre owners and restaurant operators, the town council refused to pass the ordinance, claiming it might be unconstitutional.[126]

Defeats like the proposed Sunday closing fanned fires fed by a vocal band of national "fundamentalist" leaders like William Jennings Bryan, Frank Norris and T.T. Martin. Texas evangelist Norris preached to fundamentalists that they waged nothing less than a "holy" war defending the Bible and civilization. The Northern Baptist Conference was one of the hottest battlegrounds.[127]

First Baptist joined the battle, issuing a stinging resolution following the defeat of the Sunday closing ordinance. The church had muscle, boasting a membership of almost 350. Its size and strength supported Reverend Northrup's rise in national Northern Baptist affairs. But involvement in denominational politics turned out to be a liability for Northrup at this critical time in church history.[128]

The trouble started locally when Pastor C.M. Rock of Calvary Baptist in Phoenix, openly defied a Northern Baptist directive, resigned, then turned to Southern Baptists. Crippled for decades by financial problems stemming from the Civil War, Southern Baptists stayed out of Arizona until the early twenties. Ready to move in, they welcomed Reverend Rock's overture. Rock formed a Southern Baptist church in Phoenix. Not long after, a small group left Glendale's First Baptist to form their own struggling Southern Baptist congregation. The tide roared in to Glendale in early November when Reverend Rock began nightly revival meetings. Ollie didn't attend because she had recently given birth in late October to a boy. They named him after Joe, but no one around Glendale ever knew the boy by anything other than "Junior." Certainly Joe, and perhaps Willie and Nannie, were among those who packed the house to hear Reverend Rock's "Old Time Gospel" message. Joe and other First Baptist members, fired up by Rock's words, quickly ran Reverend Northrup out, if for nothing else than guilt by association with the Northern Baptist powers. Reverend Northrup's nine years in Glendale were over without so much as a last sermon or the usual complimentary editorial in the town paper. First Baptist hired Revered Ed Butler. People flocked to hear the new pastor.[129]

The ouster couldn't have been a big shock to Northrup. After all, he had just returned from Northern Baptist headquarters, a focal point of the debate between fundamentalism and modernism. Both were complex and changing views of religion and God. One scholar defined modernism as "the adaptation of religious ideas to modern culture," including Darwinism, and the "New Theology." That thinking was anathema to fundamentalists who viewed the Bible as the authority and modern culture as a threat to civilization.[130]

Kate needed to sandwich in two family weddings before Reverend Northrup left. Henry married in a small wedding in Kate's parlor.

Marguritte's marriage gave Kate the opportunity to stage the social affair she'd hoped to put on for her other girls. Ollie attended Marguritte's wedding, feeling fit and showing off her newborn. Two weeks later, she, Kate, Leolia and Henry's new wife spent the day at Fannie's. It felt good to be back in the fold again, but ten days later, Ollie was so sick with flu that Kate went to the farm to help Nannie nurse Ollie and the baby. Joe fell ill a few days later.

Ollie and Joe missed the big commotion in town over the return of evangelist Woodie Smith. It was almost six years since Smith, along with T.T. Martin, first kicked up the baptism controversy at First Baptist. Martin moved on to join William Jennings Bryan in the anti-evolution crusade, but Smith was back preaching morals, declaring that "Glendale [is] sold out to Hell, hide and hair." Drawing heavy crowds, Smith pulled out all the stops and announced that he stood for the same high principles as the Klan. Smith found a receptive audience in Glendale, frustrated by the cotton crash and fast-moving changes since the war. Smith added the fire and a link to the Klan.[131]

The new Klan rolled into Phoenix in early 1921. Within months, organizers enlisted over 250 supporters, with 800 statewide. The Klan made its presence known in Glendale with a blazing cross atop a building in town a few months after Smith's visit. Members enjoyed appearing, fully hooded, at a few church services. At its height in 1923, the Klan in Glendale could count on a full house for its speakers and unwavering support for its Bible memorizing project in the elementary school.[132]

An obvious goal was to impact politics. But too much negative press, nationally and locally, brought defeats at the polls and waning support. Calling itself the "Citizens Party Ticket," the Glendale Klan launched an aggressive campaign in 1924 to take over the city's council. Across the country, the Ku Klux Klan sought political control at the national, state and town levels with a platform calling for law and order, the return of strict morality and state control of all schools. Locally, the Klan stressed its phenomenal growth and strength. It was too much for voters. The Klan lost handily across the state and most of the nation.[133]

Spring 1923 brought a much needed upturn. Banks were in their best condition since the cotton crash. Memory of the crash was too fresh for Joe to jump back into cotton, but many others, including Luther, took the risk and made good money. Their profits so enthralled others again with cotton's promise that Valley farmers planted 98,000 acres that fall. Joe and Luther both felt so secure they took off for the first time and drove their wives, Ollie and Rebecca, and young boys on the first of what would be many motor trips up the windy, treacherous and always dusty road over Roosevelt Dam and into the mountains to visit Marguritte and Ham on the Mogollon Rim. Once at the ranch, Joe and Luther rode a little with Ham and his crew in the rugged timbered canyons, made repairs around the ranch yard or sat and talked a bit. Ollie and Rebecca helped Marguritte cook for the hands and put up vegetables and tomatoes from the garden. There was always plenty to do at the OW Ranch, but the cool mountain air, sudden afternoon rainstorms and camaraderie were a refreshing break.[134]

Hoping to manufacture a positive climate, Glendale's town paper declared "An Era of Unprecedented Prosperity" during the summer of 1924. The statement had some merit. Farmers cut a bumper crop of hay. Cotton was high and plentiful. Joe and Ollie, back in cotton, breathed a little. Later in the summer, when the bolls hung heavy, farmers further south defied Governor Hunt's order to destroy nine thousand acres to prevent the spread of boll weevil. Farmers were ready to sue if the governor came closer. Farmers produced nearly 108,000 bales, leading bankers, mayors and writers to warn again against the foolishness of one crop farming. Cantaloupe growers shipped 50 percent more than in the year before, almost one million in a single day.[135]

While new transplants eagerly grabbed undeveloped land around the outskirts of the Valley, a few were fortunate to buy developed land. The eighty-acre farm directly across the road from the Haley's was for sale. It was a good farm, with a big house sporting glass windows, an indoor bathroom and solar water heating. An olive grove surrounded by date palms and fig trees stood between the house and the road. The place was listed at just over $100 an acre, Joe heard some of the men say down at the Flour and Feed.[136]

He drove off on his way to town one afternoon, not long after the neighboring farm sold and the previous owners moved out. Ollie and Nannie stood in the kitchen together, finishing up some canning, while Junior napped and Willie tinkered with a repair near the tool shed. It was a nice afternoon, still warm, though not as hot as some. Things were quiet, peaceful. A light breeze fluttered through the leaves of the ash trees in the south lawn and into the kitchen through the open screens, cooling the women standing over the hot wood stove. Lost in quiet reverie, it took Ollie a moment to react to the terrible sound coming from the direction of the road. Dropping the ladle, she took off running across the kitchen, out of the screen door and through the yard. Cries and screams pierced the air. It wasn't until Ollie turned onto the tree-lined road itself that she saw the mess: two cars, one tipped on its side in the ditch full of water, five or six children clamoring for a way out. It was difficult for Ollie to get her bearings and figure out where she was needed most.

Joe's automobile sat in the middle of the road, essentially unharmed, but Ollie saw instantly that the situation with Joe was volatile. There he was, on his feet, cursing and yelling, every muscle taut, the veins in his neck popping and his arms ready to throw a punch that would send the drenched man across from him to the ground. The man was a stranger to Ollie and as angry as Joe, if curses told the tale. From what he said, Ollie gathered Joe ran the man off the road just as the man was about to turn into his new place across the road from the Haleys. Joe, of course, denied the allegation with everything he had.

Ollie knew Joe needed to be pulled off, but the cries of the children in the ditch were more urgent. Running to the ditch bank, she realized the car also contained a woman struggling to hold on to two toddlers. Quickly getting a secure foothold, Ollie reached down as the woman handed up first one, then the other, of the small children.

Nannie was not far behind. Seeing Ollie helping the children, Nannie made a beeline for Joe. She had him high-tailing it back to his farm for the team of horses to pull the strangers' auto out of ditch in no time.

Fortunately, no one was hurt in the accident that afternoon. Ollie got Callie and the seven children out of the submerged vehicle and then quickly ran back to the house to gather sheets and towels and check on Junior. Still sleeping, he lay peacefully under Willie's watchful eye.

Nannie and Ollie helped Callie and her children unload belongings and haul them up to the McAllisters' new home. With the family somewhat settled, the two Haley women scrambled back across the road to pull out all the fixings for a welcome dinner for the two families, which they shared well into the evening. Joe and "Mr. Mac" begrudgingly eyed one another as Callie and the children told how the McAllisters came from Texas, with a stint of homesteading and ranching in New Mexico. They'd survived a hard winter snowed in at Pie Town during the influenza epidemic, but many of their fellow homesteaders did not. The McAllisters took on several orphan children until distant relatives could arrive. The experience haunted Callie.

The McAllisters' two older boys arrived by train a few days later with the dairy herd and the family's belongings. Mr. McAllister and his boys had their dairy set up within days. By that time, the women and children of the McAllister and Haley families had worn a path between the two houses. The rhythm of life on the little Haley farm was never again the same.[137]

A farmer driving a tractor through cotton, n.d. *Courtesy of the Glendale Arizona Historical Society*.

5

THE FARMER PROBLEM

The Salt River is a tributary. Beginning in the mountains northeast of the Valley, it takes on snowmelt as it cascades down canyons, picking up water from the Verde River and smaller streams. In the old days, before farmers stored every drop of the river's water behind mammoth dams, it flowed through the Salt River Valley, often flooding, before joining the Gila River in the far West Valley. While the Colorado is the "Big" river of the southwest, the Gila plays second fiddle to none in Arizona. Beginning in the Black Range of New Mexico, the Gila takes a 650 mile ride west through barren desert to the area around Yuma and the Mexican Delta, where it joins the Colorado River. In its course, the Gila drains a watershed of 60,000 square miles.[138]

Land along the Gila was home to the Akimel O'odham (which translates to "river people") who used river water for centuries to irrigate crops. By the mid-nineteenth century, they cultivated between 13,000 and 28,000 acres, but soon saw water flow dwindle when white settlers and miners in the mountains constructed checks further up on the river. The checks were soon followed by more permanent canals. The Akimel O'odham appealed to the government in the late 1900s. The solution proposed was to build a large dam to store and distribute water. Building the first federally constructed dam on the Gila (San Carlos) instead of the Salt was an active, competitive idea in the early rounds of Salt River dam negotiations. When the Gila plan failed, the government built wells as compensation.[139]

While the Salt River Valley flourished, land dependent upon the Gila languished. Representative Carl Hayden took up the cause of a dam on the Gila in 1912, pushing to put the San Carlos Dam back on the federal government's now-loaded dam building docket. By 1925, the federal government had completed twenty-nine major irrigation projects, opening up several million acres to irrigation. Finally, Congress passed authorization for the San Carlos Dam. The project was to serve eighty thousand acres. Water was first to benefit the Akimel O'odham, with a full fifty thousand acres. The remainder could serve other farmers.[140]

Those other farmers were chomping at the bit to grow the cash crop: cotton. Farmers around the state produced over 108,000 bales in 1924—40,000 more than the year before, netting an average of $108 per acre. There was a brief time in 1924 when Ollie and Joe thought they were finally out of the woods. They paid off the mortgage and even bought ten more acres on the lateral directly west of their land. Cotton euphoria was so great that bankers and chamber of commerce men held a banquet in Phoenix to celebrate, broadcasting the proceedings live across the state.[141]

Cotton wasn't the only crop to prosper. It was the dairy bonanza that drew the McAllisters to the Valley. Farmers milked approximately twenty-five thousand head again; consumer demand was spurred by confidence in higher milk standards. Summer's slow, steady rains yielded bumper field crops in alfalfa, too. Valley lettuce growers shipped two thousand carloads east while Glendale's melon crop had an estimated value of over $2 million.[142]

Bounty had its down side, though. It was soon evident the additional ten acres were a burden on Ollie, especially when Joe refused to buy a tractor. He disliked machines as much as Ollie hated working horses, especially when she was pregnant. Nannie wrote folks back in Missouri during the fall of 1925 that "Ollie is looking for the stork any time after the first of the year, but don't say a word about it in your letters for she wants to surprise you." Ollie's baby girl, Genevieve, arrived right on schedule.[143]

There was no time for Ollie to "lay in" after this birth, with customers at the farmers' market buying up all the produce she could provide. Nannie brought the baby to the fields for Ollie to nurse, three-year-old Junior in tow. Joe and Ollie worked to get the ground ready and crops planted for another good year. Willie helped Ollie some with the truck garden and orchard and tended the chickens and hog. Nannie cared for the children, did all the housework and churned butter for sale. Years later Ollie would say her greatest regret was not raising her little children herself. Still, despite the workload, Ollie and Nannie found time to dash to the McAllisters', often chasing after Junior. He slipped across the road to play with Carroll and Susan every chance he got. Pursuing their runaway, Ollie or Nannie always grabbed a quick cup of coffee with Callie, building deep friendships.[144]

Mealtimes were more hectic with two children, but still the center of both business and family life. Someone entertained Junior while Ollie tended her baby for a bit. Another passed Nannie's biscuits or cornbread. Adults read the morning or afternoon paper, commenting on the funnies, ads and headlines. All four closely followed news the summer of 1925 as William Jennings Bryan took on liberal modernists in what came to be called the "Monkey Trial." The Dayton, Tennessee, court scene pitted fundamentalists, represented by Bryan, against modernists, represented by famed jurist, Clarence Darrow, over the issue of teaching evolution in high school biology. The Haleys weren't so much interested in evolution as they were the frequent mention of T.T. Martin, the evangelist well known locally for kicking up the immersion baptism controversy at First Baptist, Glendale years before. That old conflict came to a head the following winter.[145]

The first Sunday of February 1926 began like any other for First Baptist. Attendance pushed four hundred as adults and children clamored into the auditorium for the morning service. The choir led the congregation in a few familiar hymns. Parents settled restless children as Reverend Butler rose behind the podium.[146]

"My dear people," the beloved pastor began. "I find myself facing conditions, the serious extent of which I did not fully realize until a few days ago."

Reverend Butler paused, seeing every eye gravely fixed upon his. "These conditions are the modernistic and unbaptistic practices of a large number of the Northern Baptist Convention," he nearly shouted.

> *I have known for some years that some of the churches of the North Baptist Convention receive alien immersion and practice open communion, but I did not know until I read The Watchman Examiner of January 21, this year, that the Northern Baptist Convention has taken into their denominational fellowship bodily the Free Baptists, knowing that the said Free Baptists received people into their membership who were sprinkled for baptism, and those who objected were taken without any baptism at all. Also that there are several hundred other churches in the Northern Baptist Convention that are doing the same thing. I must sever my connection with the Northern Baptist Convention. For no one can affiliate with the convention and not be a party to the work thereof. I must obey God. I have told you the whole truth and I leave it in your hands to do as you think is your duty toward God.*

A good number of the stunned congregation gathered at Kate Brooks's to eat and discuss which way to turn. Leaving meant breaking fellowship and abandoning old friendships. Voices were raised and tempers were on edge, but the group ended with a unanimous decision: they would follow Butler. The week brought a flurry of discussions. The outcome was the formation of a new church. Approximately 140 members withdrew from First Baptist to form Calvary Southern Baptist Church, Glendale. The thirty members of the existing Glendale First Southern Baptist Church disbanded and joined the new fellowship. The church called Reverend Butler as its pastor. Within days, he began publication of his *Doctrinal Trumpet* to expose the errors within the Northern Baptist Church. Victor Brooks's new wife, Helen, was one of the first to be baptized, full immersion, in the new Southern Baptist church.[147]

Some gained and some lost in the move. Joe was soon a deacon, teacher and trusted treasurer. Kate, however, never regained her position. While she attended Calvary on Sundays, she redirected her energy toward her lodge instead.

The church split weighed heavily on Ollie, already burdened with the new baby and the workload. Nannie had never seen her so low. What the young mother needed, Nannie figured, was something that was just hers. The question was: what? The answer came early in the spring when several women approached Ollie to pitch for a new Glendale baseball team as part of the Valley Business Women's league. When Ollie dismissed the idea, Nannie got to work behind the scenes. The biggest hurdle, of course, was Joe. Nannie pulled out all of the stops, winning his support as well as a promise to pick up the work Ollie missed while playing. Nannie then turned to Ollie. Nannie would get dinner early on game days so she, Ollie and the two children could leave before noon. Nannie would care for Junior and the baby in the stands so Ollie could nurse while she wasn't pitching. Nannie saw the sparkle in Ollie's eyes as she explained the plan, knocking down each of Ollie's objections before it was voiced. They would be home before the milking, Nannie explained confidently. If not, Joe would get things started.

Twelve years off the mound, plowing and milking, took nothing from Ollie's arm. Her eyes were as sharp as ever. Week after week, Ollie, Nannie and the children rushed off midday. The effort didn't go down in history. Women's teams at the state university and college received scant enough coverage. Reporters and cameras completely ignored the more amateur teams like Ollie's.

One young man was determined to give Ollie's team a bit of their due. Glendale's star male player, Elton Yancy, invited the women's team to a picnic and informal game with the state champion, Glendale Cardinals. The high school boys' baseball team was back on top. Yancy did it all. Topping his high school career off, the now-famed pitcher hit a home run out of the ballpark to send Glendale to the semifinals. Glendale went on to Tucson for the finals, making the whole thing look as easy as pie. Horns blasted all the way across the Valley as Glendale heralded the triumphant team. Yancy and the 1923–26 Cardinals went down in history: hometown legends with Elton Yancy, the state's all-time strike-out king to this day.[148]

Pitching was a much-needed tonic for Ollie. Baseball fever grew as more organizations created teams. The game took on international import when Glendale's Greys traveled to Nogales. Joe and Ollie caught a number of games for various teams around Glendale, taking Junior and meeting up

The Glendale Union High School boys' baseball team, state champions in 1923 and 1926. Front row, left to right: Cliff Pullins, Merle Heatwole, Frank Sancet, Oyer Dugger. Middle row, left to right: Bill Betts, Bert Pullins, Stan Novis. Back row, left to right: Willis Moore, Elton Yancy, Bill Steinburger, Alex Maldonado, Coach Tussey. *Courtesy of the Glendale Arizona Historical Society.*

The First Southern Baptist Church of Glendale. n.d. *Courtesy of the author*.

with Luther, Rebecca and their son, Alden, at the games. Junior idolized his cousin who was already a strong baseball player.[149]

Good times continued in the spring of 1926. Money flowed into local banks and the state's travel industry boomed. Closer to home, Calvary Baptist continued to grow, with attendance hitting over three hundred in its first six months. The tremendous growth accelerated the church's building plans.

Many farmers barely paid their bills, however. Nationally, farmers' buying power stagnated under the twin burdens of low prices for agricultural goods and rising farm debt. Farm spokesmen tried to convince businessmen and the general public that the "Farmers' Problem" imperiled the stability of the entire economic system, but their song fell mostly on deaf ears. Farmers put the blame on Secretary of Commerce and future President, Herbert Hoover. Hoover stood firm on minimal government intervention in the economy, while farm lobbies called for price supports and high tariffs.[150]

Born Democrats, Joe and Ollie wouldn't support Herbert Hoover if he backed price supports, the tariff, stiffer regulations of railroads and walked on water besides. That Hoover did not back a single one of the farmers' proposals turned Joe and Ollie's natural opposition for a Republican into outright disgust. Hoover's stubborn disregard for the farmers' plight, and the suffering later on, multiplied that disgust into blind hatred for all things Hoover.

The bottom fell out of the cotton market again in the fall of 1926. The Arizona Cotton Growers' Association advised farmers to hold out for a better price and pressured banks to relieve farmers' distress with short-term loans. Joe and Ollie's bank account ran dry long before any relief reached it. They missed mortgage payments and scrambled to save the farm from foreclosure. It was 1920 all over again.[151]

Joe couldn't help but think of the Glendale farmers making a killing that very day in cantaloupes and lettuce. Glendale's new ice plant opened up eastern markets, assuring those farmers both profits and futures. But melon and lettuce farming took know-how and equipment Joe didn't have.[152]

Stress and worry took their toll on all who lived in that little house. Joe flew off the handle over almost anything, Nannie's power over his temper ebbing. Ollie tried to keep Junior out of his daddy's path, but it wasn't always possible. Joe lashed out at the small boy, adding to Ollie's share of the care and worry over the farm. At least Ollie could talk things out with Callie McAllister. The McAllisters' house was a delightful diversion for more than just Junior. Callie listened sympathetically to Ollie before offering other perspectives, perhaps coaxing Ollie to worry less about the ups and downs of farming and foreclosure threats. Gathering her boy, Ollie walked back

A man irrigating lettuce. *Courtesy of the Glendale Arizona Historical Society.*

81

across the road from these visits calmer until one summer day when she came home with more worry than she took. Seven-year-old Carroll McAllister had a high fever. The doctor stopped by the Haley's after seeing Carroll that afternoon. A hot flash of terror tore right through Ollie when the doctor said "infantile paralysis." Ollie ached for her friends and the sick little boy she loved. She filled with fear at the thought that Junior, too, would take sick with the dreaded killer. Those fears grew stronger when news came a week later that Carroll's six-year-old sister, Susan, was down with the fever. The doctor counseled Ollie and Nannie to watch Junior closely for symptoms. The threat was real.

The McAllisters' quarantine compounded Ollie's fear and sorrow. Joe helped other neighbors with the McAllisters' milking. Ollie and Nannie delivered food to the quarantine box, but it wasn't enough. They all felt helpless. Four-year-old Junior, full of love and energy, didn't understand why he couldn't play with his friends. Ollie and Nannie watched constantly to keep him from running across the road like he'd done so many joyful times before. Ollie's boy stayed well, though always sad and uncomprehending about his friends.[153]

News came that Carroll died after several days of suffering. Susan was gone a week later. Still quarantined, the McAllisters could not attend their children's funerals. Ollie, Nannie, Joe and Willie helped the McAllisters' extended family members arrange the services and bury the children. Authorities eventually lifted the quarantine. The older children returned to school. Mr. Mac felt old. Callie was hollow. Nannie sat with Callie over the next few weeks. There wasn't much talk, just an old woman who had walked in those shoes, touching Callie's hand and sharing painful tears. Ollie helped with the remaining McAllister children, all the while stealing glances toward the two women, wisely watching and learning from their pain in case she'd ever need to know.[154]

The deaths of the McAllister children, along with the new threat of foreclosure, put Ollie in a pit of despair like none she'd ever known. She felt tired and depressed for weeks. It was the small things that finally brought her out of the gloom. The birth of Victor and Helen's son, Dickie, came as an unexpected joy for Ollie. There was nothing like a baby to melt Ollie's heart. Baseball could nearly do the same. She began spending time every evening catching and throwing balls with Junior. He already knew the fundamentals of the game and had a strong arm. Over the years, Ollie would train him with all the devotion of a famed professional molding a once-in-a-lifetime champ.

Ollie Haley and her children, circa 1928. *Courtesy of the author.*

The year closed with Joe and Ollie planting conservatively, out of the cotton business again. They weighed expenditures and wasted nothing. The experience would prove good training in the troubled future, but the decision to stay out of cotton looked foolish as another heady cotton boom took hold during the summer of 1927.[155]

Joe felt like a dumb fool as he listened to cotton farmers down at the Flour and Feed late that summer brag about the fortunes they expected to make on the crop ready to pick. Luther was more humble, but he, too, stood to make a killing. Joe and Ollie netted decent profits with their dairy, alfalfa and grains, but it was no fortune. With the bills paid, tensions eased. Ollie relaxed a bit, except when she went across the road to visit poor Callie. "Grief has overtaken her," Nannie said often, shaking her head in sad resignation.

Ollie and Nannie poured their creative energy into dressing the children for Sunday. Nannie made Junior's little suits. Ollie embroidered fine cotton for Genevieve's frilly dresses and tied her hair in layers of ringlets every Saturday night. No matter how much she prepared, however, it seemed Ollie was always in a rush on Sunday mornings. She figured she'd won the battle if she could just get the milking done, breakfast eaten, children dressed, hair in place, brassiere and stockings pulled on and every one out the door without a confrontation with Joe over the time.

She was already running late that Sunday morning when Rebecca cornered her on the stairs at church and whispered there was a problem concerning Fannie. The rest would have to wait until after church. There were too many big ears there.

Ollie imagined a number of terrible things over the next three hours. She hadn't seen Fannie in some time. It was a long distance to Glendale for Fannie since Leo bought the new farm east of Phoenix. Fannie and Leo hadn't been to church since moving there in the spring, though Leo was around town some with his band. Jack drove out to see Fannie regularly, but he was always tight-lipped, covering real news with jokes and pranks.

Rebecca set out a plentiful Sunday dinner straight from her large garden. Filled up, Luther and Joe headed for the porch for the little Sunday nap they regarded as their privilege. Alden occupied Junior with throwing baseballs while Rebecca's two girls played under the big tree. Ollie put Genevieve down for a nap before rejoining Rebecca in the kitchen.

Rebecca started to speak. Overcome, she leaned against the counter in tears. It wasn't long before both sisters abandoned the dishes and sat at the kitchen table, heads in their hands; the tale Rebecca told was that bad.

Leo was in love with his worker's wife and wanted a divorce. The two sisters cried and screamed so loud Rebecca's young girls heard them clearly out in the yard.

"Oh, I rue the day I ever brought that man home," Becky cried. "Fannie would never have met him if I hadn't let him court me first."[156]

"Becky, it isn't your fault. You know that. Fannie has a mind of her own," Ollie responded in an attempt to comfort her sister.

"That isn't all," Becky cried, going on to explain that Leo planned to force Fannie's hand by putting her—five months pregnant—and three of the four little girls out on a desert homestead near Casa Grande to prove a claim he was entitled to as a war veteran. Kate would keep the oldest child so she could attend school. All Fannie had to do was live in the small one room house Leo built. He would come every two weeks with food and water.[157]

"Fannie can't live in the middle of the desert with three little children and a baby on the way!" Ollie screamed and cursed.

Joe Haley Jr. and Genevieve Haley, 1928. *Courtesy of the author.*

"Well, that's what she is going to do," Rebecca yelled, hitting the table so hard the dishes shook.[158]

Fannie's little girls thought the trip to their new home was a great adventure. The girls' daddy nearly flew over the new dirt highway to Casa Grande, fifty miles south of Phoenix. Along the way, Fannie told the children that living in their new house would be like camping. The house, they discovered, was one small room made of wood and set up on pilings to keep desert creatures like rattlesnakes, scorpions, Gila monsters, coyotes and pesky quail from walking right in. Leo made the roof of palm fronds from neighbors' trees, the door a gunny sack. There was a matching outhouse. Plenty of homesteaders around Casa Grande started out in houses something like Fannie's, despite infestations of rabbits, skunks and rattlesnakes. Fannie's closest neighbors were a mile down the road, the town several miles farther.[159]

Scattered around the dry desert were a few fields of cotton, alfalfa and grains, fed by water pumped from wells. That was all about to change with water from the Coolidge Dam. Though the dam didn't fill completely until

1941, the area became the cotton mecca of Arizona during the 1930s and '40s, outpacing the rest of the state.[160]

Leo's homestead land was native desert, waiting for someone's back-breaking labor to clear the stumps and cacti and dig the ditches in preparation for the irrigation soon to come. Leo didn't intend on being that someone. He was the speculator. He planned to prove the claim and then cash in on Casa Grande's big boom. The next man could do the work.[161]

The plan was right in line with the thinking of the day. Just about everyone believed Casa Grande Valley's time was right around the corner. Developers grabbed all the land they could, advertising colonization efforts to attract thousands of new farm families. Local merchants expanded in anticipation of the boom. There was even a housing shortage in town. Right place, right time.[162]

While the Gila River project moved forward, Arizona's position on the Colorado weakened. With Arizona's refusal to ratify the compact, Upper Basin states (New Mexico, Colorado, Utah and Wyoming) pushed for a six-state ratification, opening the door for support of the big dam at Boulder Canyon. California Representative Swing and Senator Johnson introduced a joint bill for the construction of Boulder Dam in 1923, adding to the animosity in Arizona. Hunt, on the other hand, lobbied within Arizona for a dam to be built by the state at Glen Canyon in the far northeast corner of the state.

Hunt won re-election in both 1924 and '26, continuing his active opposition to the compact and Swing-Johnson Bill. Nonetheless, the Boulder Canyon Act became law in 1924, paving the way for start of the construction on the dam. While the bill called for the federal government to build the dam, it did not specify whether or not the government would produce or distribute the power. Several interests vied for control within Arizona. The Salt River Water Users' Association lobbied for sole position.

George W.P. Hunt was defeated at the polls in 1928, ushering in a change of strategy. Focus on the Boulder Canyon Dam had taken attention away from the Gila River and its contributions to allocations of the Colorado for only a while. The Gila would be center stage again in the future.[163]

Fannie was more concerned with the late August heat and settling her girls in on the homestead than the politics of dams. It didn't take her long to get into her new routine. With little fresh food, cooking was simple. With water in short supply, Fannie relaxed her cleanliness standards. That left long days with not much to do but entertain her three little girls, wait out her pregnancy and deal with occasional creature encounters like a "big spotty monster" in the outhouse. Fannie managed to capture the Gila monster safely and move it off far enough away to give her some peace of mind. She drew especially on her memories of childhood in the little house next to the Grand Canal, teaching her girls the games she'd played with her own sisters. Her girls, in turn, felt safe and secure.[164]

She was less successful with her own mother and sisters. Kate and Jack came to visit and size up Fannie's situation just a couple of weeks after she and the girls settled in. Kate begged Fannie to go back to town with them, but Fannie stood firm. She and the girls were fine. They all just needed to have faith that her husband would see what was right. She came into town to give birth to a healthy boy. Nothing her mother or sisters said could keep her from returning to the desert.

Farmers all around Fannie furiously cleared canals and ditches the spring of 1928 in anticipation of the first filling of the new dam. Prosperity looked like a sure thing throughout Arizona farmlands. Production exploded in almost every crop. In the Salt River Valley, Glendale growers shipped 637 carloads of cantaloupes in less than two weeks. Agriculture officials urged residents to grow citrus on every vacant spot of ground. Bankers, businessmen and the Salt River Valley Water Users' Association continued to push the small farm and diversification theme as the sure formula for success for both farmers and the Valley. A Glendale farmer with thirty acres was said to net $150 per acre with a combination of cotton, alfalfa, turkeys and chickens. The Water Users' optimistically launched a campaign to attract eight thousand farm families to additional land to be opened up in the West Valley, claiming development would increase Valley farm production by $20 million to over $50 million annually.[165]

Prosperity drove Arizonans to vote with most of the nation for Herbert Hoover for President. Hoover offered nothing new for farmers, but continued to stress cooperatives and elimination of waste. Joe and Ollie had nothing to do with Hoover, but rode the wave of prosperity and optimism, purchasing another twenty acres, raising their total to fifty acres. But the bad times left their mark. Never again would Joe and Ollie put all of their hope in cotton.

Refusing to mechanize forced them to take on more hands. They enlisted Junior, almost seven, to work when he wasn't in school. Joe and Ollie kept up with the dairy themselves, hiring help for field work. The majority of available workers were Mexican nationals or Mexican Americans. That was a problem.

Neither Joe nor Ollie brought skill to the task of managing their workers. Growing up in the Valley, Ollie was sheltered from contact with Spanish-speaking people and their culture. Newer to the Valley, Joe had even less experience. Thrust suddenly into the role of "boss," he approached the position as an Old South overseer, masking his insecurities with assumptions of authority, laying his prejudices bare. The McAllisters often intervened when language was a problem, but conflicts between Joe and his laborers were frequent.[166]

Glendale responded to the new wave of prosperity with capital improvements. The first order of business was cement sidewalks. Civic groups organized a campaign to plant trees and clean up and paint the town. Citizens' efforts to build a public swimming pool finally paid off. Glendale's golf enthusiasts opened a small course north of town.[167]

Ollie found it hard to enjoy the bounty. Fannie seldom left her mind. Driving the plow behind the two horses, each day hotter than the last, Ollie's thoughts turned to Fannie in the little house on the desert, waiting out the midday glare. It wasn't hard to imagine the baby cranky, the little girls restless in the heat. How did Fannie believe that everything was going to be all right?

The situation came to a head late that spring. Leo made his decision. He wanted a divorce. Fannie had prepared for this. "No," she replied softly when Leo asked. A quiet woman of few words, she didn't feel the need to offer much explanation. Silently, though, Fannie had to wonder how much longer she could hold out.

Family folklore says the break came in a vision. Leo dreamed his mother, dead for many years, sat at the foot of his bed more alive than Leo himself felt right then. Mrs. Varney knew the problem and had a few things to say. The apparition got right into his face, pronouncing a clear warning. "Do not divorce Fannie," she said, "or the result will be disaster."

Leo woke from the sleep, haunted by what he'd dreamed. Daylight brought no peace. Finally, he came to Fannie. He'd do as his mother bid. He'd come back.[168]

A relieved Kate hosted a large Fourth of July celebration that included Fannie and Leo, along with a roster of family and friends. The year had taken its toll, though. Kate entered the hospital with heart problems and complications from diabetes just two weeks later. Fannie stayed on the homestead through August to finish proving the claim. Doing so was no easy task. Leo sold the land four years later at the heart of the Depression for tax reasons.[169]

Leo had a plan for a fresh start. He'd take his family back to Missouri, his birth state. The news hit Ollie and Rebecca like a ton of bricks.

"This is crap, Rebecca, and you know it," Ollie declared, again within range of young ears. "Mama is as good as dead."

The two sisters didn't spare any sentiment in laying that argument right on Fannie. The words surely stung. In the end, though, Fannie left. Not long after, Leolia, Kate and Jack's youngest, packed to go to her first teaching job in the mining district east of the Valley.[170]

The final days of the decade flew by quickly. Pundits and politicians promised a better time in the new decade, but Ollie had mixed feelings. Certainly, she'd gained a great deal over the last ten years, but she'd lost, too. Nannie was winding down. Always so in charge, Nannie began asking Ollie what to cook, when to clean. Most women would welcome coming to power in their own home. Not Ollie. She knew what it meant.

The passing of the McAllister children left a hole in everyone around. Mr. Mac and Callie were shadows of themselves. Finally, they wrote to one of the older boys, Ed, married and living in Texas, asking him to come and help with the farm. Duty bound, Ed and his wife, LouEdna, changed plans and came home to Glendale with their toddler son, TomEd.

"Ollie was a godsend to me," LouEdna recalled of her good friend seventy years later.[171]

6

FEAR ITSELF

Joe and Ollie drove past fields of ripe cotton on a glorious Saturday morning. The worn car kicked up dust on the lateral roads west of Glendale, despite Joe's slow pace. He always looked more at the fields than the road, checking to see which farmers planted straight rows and kept their fields without a hint of weeds. Farmers had much at stake in the white bolls hanging heavy that morning. While every crop, from cantaloupes to wheat, demanded devotion, cotton upped the ante. It was the farmers' casino, all glitz and promise, luring even the righteous to risk it all. One season of cotton profit was all it took to convince a man that cotton was the way to heaven.

Like all novice gamblers, cotton farmers never expected to lose. But cotton never *slipped*, it *crashed*, taking those new to the game with it. The first catastrophe for Arizona farmers was the crash in 1920 when Egypt's pent up supply, as well the United States government's suddenly released reserves, shut out that year's crop, bankrupting farmers across the country. Joe Haley struggled to keep his twenty acres, while Glendale Russians' dream of the good life in America disintegrated overnight. Four years later, Joe was not only back in the game, but heady with cotton's profits again. With the farm paid off, he and Ollie even expanded. Cotton crashed again. They barely pulled out before foreclosure that time.[172]

It was probably embarrassment as much as financial loss that kept Joe and Ollie from jumping all the way into cotton after that. Joe hated playing the fool, even though every player walked away with nothing at one time or another in the cotton game. In 1927, Joe watched from the sidelines as Luther and every other cotton farmer around reeled in another fortune from cotton. Joe and Ollie paid the bills, took vegetables to market every week, along with the butter Nannie churned, and repaired whatever broke or wore out. It was existence but not cotton jubilee.[173]

Many around the Salt River Valley were confident the stock market crash of 1929 would have little effect on them. Cotton farmers, after all, didn't own stocks and bonds, many said. Pundits pointed to the fact that the local economy was bustling. Mines reported their best year ever, pouring millions into the Valley's economy. Valley farmers continued to find strong markets for their crops. Lettuce farmers shipped over two thousand carloads, breaking the previous year's all-time high. Cantaloupes held steady. The ripple effect of mining dollars and good farm profits spurred Glendale businessmen to take on $100,000 of new construction.[174]

But cotton was a commodity living and dying on the world stage. The bottom fell out of cotton prices not long after the crash. Surpluses piled up as foreign and domestic markets shrunk. President Hoover's Federal Farm Board tried to stabilize cotton prices by buying up the surplus, but there was more cotton than dollars. Farmers who borrowed heavily to plant had their backs against the wall when loaning agencies called in loans. With stabilization a failure, the Hoover administration turned its focus back on production, attempting to get farmers to plant only for the domestic market. The plan was ridiculous. Farmers who hadn't lost their farms planted more, not less, in an attempt to compensate for low prices with greater volume. Cotton farmers produced the second largest crop in history.[175]

Joe and Ollie had a right to feel vindicated as they watched the players and braggarts struggle. What they felt instead was sorrow as they headed that Saturday morning to help Luther and Rebecca pack up their life. They were among the dozens of cotton farmers losing their farms around Glendale. Joe and Ollie both knew Luther would give them the shirt off his back, even as he lost everything. Ollie kept her face turned to the side window, hoping to hide the tears from the children wrestling in the back seat.

Minutes later, Ollie wrapped a plate in newspaper, placing it with the others in the wooden barrel for the move. The stack waiting in front of her continued to grow as Rebecca emptied cupboards. Usually talkative, the sisters worked in heavy silence, Ollie catching glimpses of Rebecca's glistening eyes each time she turned to place another pile of dishes on the table. Sighing, Rebecca said, "This is the last home we will ever own, Ollie. Luther is too broken hearted to ever try again."

Giggles from the three little girls at play in the yard outside pierced the kitchen's silence. Ollie's girl, Genevieve, loved playing with Rebecca's two, especially in the relaxed environment at Rebecca and Luther's. The girls found less supervision with Luther and Joe busy packing up tools in the barn. Alden and Junior were supposed to help the men some, but seemed instead to spend more time catching balls and harassing their sisters.[176]

Talk in the barn focused on the villain of the day: President Herbert Hoover. Farmers like Luther were losing everything. Luther and Joe complained to one another while President Hoover stonewalled farmers. Hoover's stabilization, coop and marketing plans made Luther a sharecropper who was lucky to feed his family. Luther said, "'Let 'em eat cake.' Mr. Hoover says, Joe. We've got our own French import, right here, running our government."[177]

Rebecca and Luther thought their children oblivious to what was happening. Years later, Bobbe, the youngest, recalled her parents' despair, their valiant efforts to shield the three, to make the sharecropper's rented house livable after leaving the house Rebecca so lovingly maintained.[178]

Cotton's troubles spread to other sectors around Glendale. The first crack appeared when Glendale's Bank of Commerce locked its doors in late April 1930. The town's optimism soon gave way to pep talks. "Take that padlock off your purse." "Spend now, buy now and start the wheels of industry," Glendale's merchants urged with every edition of the town's newspaper.[179]

Joe and Ollie were well-seasoned travelers on the relentless paths of worry and fear. Sleepless nights, quitclaim maneuvers and years of working their bodies to the bone made them tired but wise. Ignoring the pleas to spend, they tightened their belts and let the hired help go. The load got heavier when Willie died around Christmas 1930. Willie never made it home to see his mighty river again. They buried him in the desert cemetery next to his son, Don.[180]

The stringent economy and loss pushed Joe and Ollie to rely more on Junior. He was old enough now, they thought, to carry some of the milking and fieldwork, but closer contact brought more conflict between Joe and his son. Junior daydreamed and forgot to close the gate or clean the milk pails thoroughly, misdeeds that brought the worst out in Joe. Ollie, for all her fire, was helpless in the face of Joe's rages against the boy. Nannie was no longer an effective buffer. The best Ollie could do was to urge the boy to take his responsibilities seriously and do better at his chores. Junior grew up thinking he never did a good enough job.[181]

The boy took his own anger out at school. He was a thorn in the flesh of every tightly coiffed and corseted teacher hell bent on maintaining order at the country school full of rough and tumble farm kids and transients. Spitballs, pranks, fighting and ditching: Junior was expert at every offense. Ollie channeled some of Junior's energy with a paper route. Mornings and afternoons, he pedaled miles of unpaved country roads, making friends with most of the dogs that ran unleashed. Saturday mornings, he pedaled to town to pay his bill at the newspaper office and visit Victor, two pints of ice cream in hand.

Rebecca and Luther settled onto eighty acres north of Glendale that Luther farmed on shares. Rebecca and Ollie scrubbed the rundown house to within an inch of its life as they dissected the lives of Kate, Papa and Fannie. Letters from Fannie were infrequent since she'd left two years before with Leo and the children to start a new life in the backwoods of Missouri. The timing of that move was poor, coinciding with the stock market crash. Both Ollie and Rebecca knew what Fannie wrote was rubbish. They thought they could read between the lines and envision the hardships.

Things were worse than imagined. After two years of deprivation, Fannie and Leo finally came back to Glendale. They settled on a farm just behind the McAllisters, not a quarter of a mile from Joe and Ollie. After all the worry and pleading, Ollie and Rebecca finally had Fannie just a stone's throw away.[182]

Glendale's churches united to remind people the church is the anchor, but churches were not immune to the times. Calvary lost hundreds of precious dollars in a bank closing. Always ambitious, Calvary's Reverend Butler threw himself into crusades for old age pensions, keeping liquor out of Glendale and stemming the tide of lawlessness sweeping the town. But attendance declined: in 1934 it was 379, down from the 1929 high of 444. The work took its toll. Reverend Butler was ill and soon retired.[183]

Depression dug deep. National commerce and industry figures for 1931 fell 20 to 30 percent below the previous year. Britain went off the gold standard, drawing down United States gold reserves. Copper prices fell below the cost of production, sending shock waves across Arizona's economy. An estimated thirty-six thousand unemployed passed through the Valley every month, migrating on to California or hunting for a warmer climate.

The influx drove the state to convert the fairgrounds into a transient camp for men. A third of Glendale's resident population received help from the Welfare Assistance League while the new Glendale ward of Latter Day Saints organized a relief committee of their own. The City Council urged Glendale to postpone construction of the new fire station. Citizens slashed school budgets. A sense of emergency permeated every aspect of daily life.[184]

New crises erupted daily. Fearful, people hoarded money, driving the banking crisis deeper. Industry stagnated. Arizona's farm production fell to just a third of what it was in 1929. With agricultural income 60 percent lower than four years earlier, farmers across the country yelled for the government to do something. Economists and regular citizens alike lobbied the federal government to fund major public works programs to put people to work. Proposals for a $5 billion program were defeated, but the seeds of the idea were planted in the public's mind, waiting for the right champion.[185]

Desperate for relief, western farmers backed Franklin Roosevelt, the Democrats' candidate for president, when he endorsed farmers' rights to price supports and government assistance with crop surpluses. Roosevelt believed, and expressed, that the roots of the Depression were in the condition of agriculture. Joe and Ollie poured their every effort into his campaign. They attended rallies, handed out leaflets to neighbors and argued Roosevelt's case with whoever would listen.[186]

It was the first election Kate missed since women got the vote in Arizona in 1912. Margaret died in the spring. Kate followed in December. All of Kate's children and grandchildren sat at the front of the church with Jack at her funeral, looking respectable. Kate would have been proud.[187]

Joe and Ollie expected one of Roosevelt's first actions in office to be help for western farmers. Instead, the president closed the nation's banks and stock exchanges for over a week to restructure the nation's banking system. People were glad to see the new president taking action, even if it meant they couldn't get at their money. Glendale merchants responded with a cash giveaway. Merchants put up only four $5 cash prizes, but the "Lucky Party" that Saturday drew the largest crowd to town since the stock market crash. Enthusiasm for the Saturday giveaways continued after banks reopened. People around Glendale needed a diversion as cantaloupes came in poorly and the school board slashed the high school's budget by 25 percent. Merchants repeated the party every Saturday for the next six months, adding more cash, radios and even an automobile.[188]

The Brooks clan held on better than most. They didn't need the government to tell them to grow more of their own food. There was always plenty to eat at their tables. The family raised hogs and steers. Rebecca, Ollie and Fannie planted larger vegetable gardens and sewed dresses out of feed sacks. Victor kept his garage afloat. Henry and Leolia held on to their jobs out of town. Marguritte and Ham continued to manage the ranch on the Mogollon Rim. Joe loaned Jack the ten-acre plot on the corner of Lateral 21 and Glendale Avenue to grow watermelons for sale, but Jack just seemed to give away his crop after Kate died.[189]

Cotton farmers didn't know what to do in the spring of 1933 except plant more cotton. Roosevelt's new government didn't pass the Agricultural Adjustment Act, spelling out reduction plans, until two months after farmers across the country seeded 11 percent more cotton than the year before. Both Joe and Luther could see the warning signs, the unwanted interference of government in their business, but like farmers everywhere, each was desperate for cash.[190]

Dairy wasn't much better off. Prepared for price controls and production reductions, Arizona farmers found themselves in a pool with "Hollywood," as they called all things California. California dairy farmers, refusing to agree to reductions, nixed the plan. The best Arizona farmers got out of the deal was more advertising.[191]

New programs spun out of Washington with amazing, and often confusing, speed in those early days of the Roosevelt Administration. Twelve thousand unemployed, including Jack Brooks, were back at work in Arizona that fall. Hard as it was, Arizona cotton farmers plowed under 22,000 acres, netting well over the $125,000 in subsidy. Few considered the impact the plow-under had on farm workers. Cotton picking usually employed the state's nineteen thousand resident workers as well as thousands of migrants.[192]

Joe and Ollie had the dairy, supplemented with alfalfa and cotton. Ollie still worked the vegetable garden for sale at the farmers' market. She spent egg and butter money for extras, particularly for Genevieve. The girl was Ollie's princess, required to do little and disciplined seldom, except one time with the cotton wagon.

Fannie's girls came to play house with Genevieve one afternoon in 1934. They had a set way of constructing their "house" under the big ash tree, using old dishes for the kitchen and pieces of wood and rope to section off rooms. The capstone of the "house" was the pretend water pump the girls made out of the old jack always laying next to the dilapidated garage. On this day, however, the jack was missing until Genevieve spotted it supporting one corner of an old wagon full of cotton. The girls needed the jack for their house, they all agreed. Together, they worked hard pulling and pushing until they freed the jack from the wagon in one loud and messy crash.

Ollie heard the wagon hit the dirt and the girls' screams. Flying out of the door, she saw the mess of white cotton bolls flying everywhere. Face red with fury, she lined those crying girls up, pulled a small branch from the ash tree just like her mama used to do and switched each one before sending Fannie's girls running home in tears. She was trying to maneuver the jack back in place when Joe came around the corner ten minutes later. Ollie's anger was nothing compared to Joe's.[193]

Not long after, the family gathered at Joe's and Ollie's on Easter Sunday for a big dinner and children's egg hunt. Twenty-six people spilled out of the small house around tables set up in the shade of the yard to eat the big ham and, of course, tamale pie. Victor and Henry cranked a freezer of ice cream, and there were enough fruit pies and cakes to send everyone's blood sugar over the limit. The children found a treasure of penny candy stashed along with their colorful Easter eggs after dinner.

Easter ribbons came untied and faces were soon smeared with that special combination of dirt and sugar unique to children left to run free. Victor and Helen's Dickie, however, found the day too much. Usually sweet and compliant, the seven-year-old was cross and whiny. Nothing was right for Dickie that Easter Sunday.

He was feverish the next day, fever climbing higher that night. The morning diagnosis was infantile paralysis. He suffered on for days. Once again, Ollie was torn between grief and panic. Her children were with Dickie just the day before. The doctor advised all of the mothers at Ollie's that Easter Sunday to keep their children home from school for the next two weeks.

Something shattered inside as Ollie watched Helen at Dickie's funeral. She'd never seen grief so raw. Helen was family, needing protection, now. How Helen found the courage to risk and love again no one knew. She was pregnant just months after Dickie's death. The women of Calvary Baptist turned out in force to throw a huge "stork shower" and show Helen how much they cared. She gave birth to another healthy boy that spring. A large picture of Dickie always sat on her dresser.[194]

The winter of 1934–35 was brutal. An estimated ten million were still unemployed, raising serious doubts about the ability of New Deal relief programs. Rays of optimism appeared, however, as spring arrived

Children swimming in a lateral of the Grand Canal. Swimming in ditches and canals was custom despite frequent warnings by county health officials of the link with infantile paralysis and other diseases, n.d. *Courtesy of the Library of Congress, Prints & Photographs Division, HAER ARIZ, 7-TEMP, 8—9.*

in Glendale. Nearly $5 billion for public works was finally a reality. The impact was dramatic, even in small towns like Glendale. Like most, Glendale had a list of projects begging for funding. Sewers were at the top. Men were at work on construction of a new system almost immediately.[195]

For a time, the shrinking economy overshadowed water on the desert, making it play second fiddle to man-made trouble. Still, the western water business moved on. The West Valley's representative to the Water Users' board of governors urged local farmers' approval of another dam on the Verde, a major tributary of the Salt River. The association had been steadily expanding its delivery of electricity generated by its dams as it lobbied for its share of Boulder Dam power. Coming on line in 1936, Boulder Dam's power plant contract was given to Southern California Edison and Los Angeles Department of Water and Power. Arizonans were irate.[196]

Arizona had continued fighting the dam from the time the Swing-Johnson Bill was passed in 1929. The state filed suit in 1930, asking the Supreme Court to declare the Boulder Canyon Act and Colorado River Compact unconstitutional on the grounds that the federal government violated Arizona's rights by proposing to build the dam within the state. In addition, the state claimed that inclusion of the Gila River in total allocations effectively reduced Arizona's water by one million acre-feet. The court threw the suit out.

Undeterred, Arizona was back at the court in 1934, this time arguing that the agreement made during Colorado River Compact negotiations in Santa Fe gave Arizona one million acre-feet more than the subsequent allotment. The court threw that appeal out on the grounds that Arizona never signed the compact.

By this time, lawyers and farmers, Republicans and Democrats alike, were steaming. Although not as flashy as George W.P. Hunt, Governor Benjamin B. Moeur was just as incensed. Unable to stop construction on Boulder Dam, Moeur called out the National Guard to block construction on Parker Dam, a diversion dam to serve California's Metropolitan Water District, to be erected 150 miles south of Boulder Dam. The Supreme Court refused to grant California an injunction, effectively giving Arizona a four month victory, until Congress acted and told Arizona to move on.[197]

Arizona changed tactics in 1944, finally signing the compact. New developments regarding Upper Basin use and the viability of a canal (which became the Central Arizona Project) from the Colorado River to the Salt River Valley pushed the decision forward. Still, it would be years before the issues between Arizona and California were decided and construction of the canal could begin. By then, estimates of water flow on which the original allocations were made were in jeopardy as weather conditions in the West changed. Still, Salt River Valley farmers believed the Colorado River water was theirs to be pumped over deserts and mountains to their crops, paid for by the federal government.

While Arizonans did not accept the concept of government control of their water or power, they had to admit agricultural price and production controls brought much needed relief. Cattle and dairy markets were the strongest they'd been in four years, while cotton prices nearly doubled per pound. With some degree of security, farmers jumped at cheap farm modernization loans. Joe planned a new, bigger hay barn. Ollie had her own priorities. Completion of the dam on the Verde River made the Valley the largest electrified farmland bloc in the world. A $74.50 stove would capitalize on the electricity and get rid of Ollie's old wood stove. She and Joe both got what they wanted, along with an indoor toilet and one of the new evaporative coolers the Water Users' Association pushed heavily that spring. Ollie's kitchen was suddenly thirty degrees cooler than previous summer afternoons. Like many, she found air conditioning went a long way to chase away pessimism.[198]

There were smaller joys. Junior's calf took top prize at the 4-H fair that spring. Joe told the boy he was real proud of him, an event that stood out in the boy's mind for a long time, helping to buffer the grief he felt in losing his steer when it was auctioned. Luther, Rebecca and Alden came to watch. Having Alden come was a special honor.[199]

Alden had Joe and Ollie under his spell. When Alden asked if Junior could travel with his Peoria baseball team to Ajo one Saturday, they said yes. Junior couldn't believe his ears.

He was up before dawn to deliver papers before leaving with Alden for the 150-mile drive. Once there, Junior sat joyfully in the stands, oblivious to the hot sun, watching the team practice before the game. As game time drew near, Peoria's coach and team grew concerned. They were short players and would have to forfeit unless more team members showed up in a hurry. That's when Alden stepped up and suggested his cousin, Junior.

"Junior?" the coach exclaimed. "Junior Haley? He's just a kid!"

"Well, I know he's young," Alden replied. "But he's good, real good. His mom taught him and you know she was good. He's got a strong arm and hits the ball pretty good. At least try him, coach. It's better than just forfeiting."

Junior saw Alden running toward him in the stands, whooping and calling his name.

"Junior, get up. You're playing center field. Hurry, come on, warm up."

Peoria lost that day, but Junior didn't embarrass Alden or the coach. In fact, at thirteen, he won himself a spot on the Peoria town team; he now played baseball with Alden, sometimes even on Sundays.[200]

Baseball and hard times seemed to go hand in hand. Every group and organization had a team and league. Glendale Grammar School's girls' softball (indoor baseball) team, with one of the McAllister girls playing, took the Salt River Valley championship in 1931 and 1935. Ollie loved to watch the girls play. Many of Glendale's women players went on to play around the country for years to come. Glendale's Greys, the men's town team, came back to life, with Elton Yancy still pitching strong. The team generated an extra dose of excitement in 1937, taking it all the way to the Central Arizona championship, only to lose to Buckeye in the ninth inning. They got their revenge the following year, shutting Buckeye out, thirteen to zip, to win the Valley tournament. The biggest news was what electricity did for the game. Families pinching pennies managed to give enough for churches and service groups to pay for the electric lights to shine almost every night of the week for dueling teams.[201]

If the improvements on their farm and Junior's new ball career weren't enough to get the Haley's out of the Depression doldrums, LouEdna McAllister had one more thing up her sleeve. As Nannie grew frailer, LouEdna pushed Joe and Ollie to take Nannie home to Missouri for a visit. She and Ed convinced Joe to hire their trusted part-time employee, Concepcion (Cion), to oversee the fields and dairy while they were gone.[202]

The trip started badly when the old Ford bit the dust grinding its way up grueling mountain roads. Ollie called her brother Henry in Williams, about forty miles east, to come and get them. As luck would have it, Henry just happened to operate a small Chevrolet dealership. He took one look at the Ford and told Joe he needed a new Chevy. That's how Joe happened to arrive back home in Missouri at the heart of the Great Depression looking like a rich man.

The Haley family, circa winter 1936. Left to right: Genevieve, Joe Jr., Ollie, Joe Sr.

101

Joe played the part without much trouble. He strutted around his old hometown talking about selling out in Arizona and buying a big farm in Missouri. Ollie knew Joe could be a braggart, but she wasn't positive he was all talk this time. She liked Joe's relations, but she sure didn't want to exchange the dry Arizona desert for the humid green of Missouri. Who knows if she said that to Joe or just kept her peace, hoping his talk was all bluster that would blow over once they headed back west? Whatever tactic Ollie used, it worked.

Back home, she visited Fannie early one morning to admire the new school dresses Fannie just finished. Later that day, a friend and her children visited Fannie and the children for noon dinner. As Fannie and the woman quilted and talked, most of the children played together right outside the door of the old frame house. Fannie's two youngest, however, played behind the house, stacking wooden crates to make a "house." As he stacked, the boy eyed a box of matches Leo left by mistake next to the trash bin earlier that morning. Fantasy and reality mixed in the child's head and he built a fire to warm his little crate box home. The crates went up in a flash, catching the dry siding of the old frame house so fast Fannie could think of nothing except to run through the burning house calling out for any child who might be indoors. Finally, someone yelled in that all the children were safe outside and that Fannie had better get out quick. The new school dresses went up in flames, along with everything else the family owned.[203]

Ollie was almost out the door after finishing her own dinner dishes when the telephone rang that afternoon with LouEdna screaming that Fannie's house was on fire.

Ollie could smell the horrible fire as soon as she got outside. One look at Ollie's face and her frightened eyes and Joe knew whatever had happened was bad.

Joe dropped his tools and turned his wife around toward the car. Telling Nannie to stay put, he sped out of the drive with Junior and Genevieve just barely making it into the back seat.

They arrived about the same time as the fire truck. The house was gone.

Ollie leaped out of the automobile and ran toward the cluster of people standing off to the side of the fire.

"My children are safe, Ollie. My children are safe," Fannie repeated as Ollie wrapped her arms around her sister. Ollie took the handkerchief tucked in her belt and wiped her sister's face. It was the only time she'd seen Fannie cry since they were young children.

The Roman Catholic "Rock" Church, Glendale, Arizona, in the 1930s. *Courtesy of the Glendale Arizona Historical Society.*

Leo and Fannie moved their family back to Missouri the next January. Jack went to help and stayed for a long time.[204]

The summer was hard for Ollie. Nannie grew weaker until she finally slipped away one hot July afternoon. Her passing brought an infusion of financial relief that marked a major turn for Joe and Ollie. Despite years of hardship, Nannie managed to maintain a sizable life insurance policy, with Joe as beneficiary. They bought the 60 acres immediately surrounding the original 20, bringing their total to 110 acres.[205]

"Maybe the Depression was a thing of the past?" people said the next winter. Works Projects Administration plans ran full steam, fixing the water works, constructing curbs and gutters and finishing the sewer system. The city moved ahead with a new library as local veterans pumped $200,000 in bonuses into the economy. The influx of federal money stimulated private expansion. Several churches or temples, including Buddhists, built or burned mortgage bonds.[206]

There was no question Joe and Ollie would vote for Roosevelt in 1936. He'd done everything they hoped for in 1932 and more. Government prices for cotton provided a security they'd never known. Dairy was strong,

Joe and Ollie Haley in an outdoor hay barn, circa 1940. *Courtesy of the author.*

demanding more alfalfa hay at reasonable prices. There was water in the ditch and electricity in the house and lighting the farmyard all night.

School closed on a sour note. Junior failed the eighth grade. Ollie was convinced he never would pass if left at the country school. That summer she pulled out all the stops to get her children in to Glendale schools. She succeeded just in time. A wave of Dust Bowl refugees hit, causing an enrollment and welfare crisis.

Cotton, lettuce and melon picking brought substantial influxes of migrant farm workers in every year, the majority Mexican nationals. School officials always worked to enroll the children, but attendance was spotty at best as children missed days and weeks to work in the fields alongside their parents. Earning seventy-five cents per one hundred pounds of cotton picked, an experienced family of five could pick four to six hundred pounds a day.[207]

Hundreds of carloads of white Dust Bowl refugees joined the usual flow of Mexican nationals pouring into the Valley. Most of the refugees had never picked cotton before. Welfare officials claimed cotton growers and labor agencies had advertised high wages and permanent employment in Valley cotton fields. Once in the Valley, whatever work refugees managed to find was not permanent. They couldn't earn enough to move on, but didn't meet the Works Project Administration's residency requirements because they usually lived in automobiles or tents. Almost 1,400 children poured into the city's grammar and high schools that fall, many shoeless and half starved. The grammar school's principal appealed to the community for support of the school milk fund and spare shoes. It was in this environment that Leolia Brooks finally found a teaching position in Glendale. She moved into Jack's house, an arrangement not always comfortable for Jack.[208]

The Fiesta Patrias, n.d. *Courtesy of the Glendale Arizona Historical Society.*

Farmers harvested bumper crops of wheat and barley, while cotton set records. Lettuce broke all records, despite the fact that farmers held back a third of acreage. Drawing inspiration from California's "Carnival of Roses," Glendale's Woman's Club staged its first Lettuce Festival, complete with an air show. Boosters hoped to grow the festival into a more elaborate spectacle. Unfortunately, the festival was poorly attended and a plane crashed into the small crowd of spectators. A more successful effort was the almost annual Mexican fiesta, complete with food and music.[209]

Alden helped with the planes that day. At seventeen, he loved airplanes. He was at the festival spotting for a young friend's aerobatic stunts. At nineteen, the friend owned his own plane and ran his own airfield, a few miles east. Alden spent every moment he could there, giving lessons and helping the friend ferry customers all over the state.[210]

Alden was just waiting for his own plane. The boy was the center of his dad's life. Still working on shares, Luther found the money to buy Alden a motorcycle and car. They were merely a prelude. Alden's plane would be delivered within the next month.

Junior, on the other hand, had a "yes, Sir," relationship with his dad. Finally, he got a little bold. The additional land demanded that Joe and Ollie make some changes. They didn't figure Junior would co-opt them. He was as big and strong as Joe now and nearly as bull-headed.

"I'm not walking behind a team of horses any more like some slave," Junior told Joe. "I'm not working anymore without a tractor."

"This is the twentieth century, Dad," Junior continued, seeing the color rise in Joe's face, "and you've got me walking behind two fool horses like we don't even know they've invented the motor. It's embarrassing when the guys see me. You can keep on doing it the old fashioned way if you want, but I'm not doing it. Buy a tractor and I'll work hard," he concluded.

Junior stood stone-still, ready for the explosion, though not quite sure what he was going to do when it came. Joe was angry but suddenly reflective. Something about the boy's stance—the tone—was familiar, resurrecting memories of Don and himself.

Remembering took the fire out. Joe knew he should punish the boy for his insolence, but even Joe could see the time had come when he needed Junior as much or more than Junior needed him.[211]

Joe also knew that Junior and a tractor weren't the entire solution. He needed full-time help with the fields and irrigating. Getting someone to work for him wouldn't be easy. Joe had a reputation among Glendale's farm workers as a difficult man, but Joe got a lucky break. Still unable to give Cion full-time work, the McAllisters convinced him to take the job with Joe and Ollie. Cion let Joe know he'd work hard, but wouldn't take much grief. He had the McAllisters to back him on that.[212]

It didn't take long for Joe and Ollie to realize Cion was a godsend. Joe joined friends for the first time that October on their annual deer hunting expedition on the North Rim of the Grand Canyon, leaving the farm to Cion and Ollie. A small, but strong man like Joe, Cion had a strong work ethic and a passionate faith. Cion stayed on for the next five years, living with his wife in a small house at the corner of the farm. During that time, he became a confidant and sounding-board for Junior. Angry, hurt or joyful, the boy ran to Cion for the calming sympathy or pat on the back he didn't get from Joe.[213]

Ollie's efforts to get Junior into Glendale schools paid off. He passed eighth grade at Glendale's grammar school and entered high school in the fall of 1938. He had reported for football practice a couple of weeks before.[214]

The story of Junior Haley's four years at Glendale High reads like the all-American soda shop script. Like many American boys, Junior's number one priority during high school was sports. He attended

Joe Haley Jr. pitching on the Glendale Union High School team, 1936–39. He created two state records that are still on the books. *Courtesy of the author.*

classes and just barely made passing grades in order to play. Football, basketball, track and baseball: Junior played it all, but, not surprisingly, his talent was for baseball. He set three state records. Ollie proudly logged her son's accomplishments in a wooden scrapbook Junior made in woodshop.[215]

Critics decried the Roosevelt administration's strategy of trying to spend the nation out of Depression, but the criticism didn't stop towns like Glendale from filing more funding requests. Glendale's latest round took in the town's changing demographics as it sought funding to build a second elementary school, as well as new structures on both grammar school and high school campuses.[216]

Alden graduated in the spring of 1937. With his college money spent on a plane and grades too poor for scholarships, he didn't go on to college. At loose ends, talk of war turned his head. War meant fighter planes. Alden gathered up books on navigation and started studying. He became a different person—focused. When news came that a small Los Angeles firm was building a plant to provide Britain 250 reconnaissance bombers, Alden could not get there fast enough. Luther tied down Alden's plane as he and Rebecca put the boy on the bus. Their time with him was over.[217]

"Peace comes of age," Glendale's merchants announced on the anniversary of Armistice Day in 1939. Hitler invaded Poland two months earlier. Finland was next, crying out for help as the Soviets bore down. Glendale turned to preparedness as the National Guard organized Glendale's new Anti-Tank unit. Seventy thousand Arizonans registered for the first peacetime draft.[218]

War preparation changed things overnight. New Deal programs were abolished, production controls gradually lifted. The United States Army moved in to the West Valley, building two air training centers: Thunderbird Field, north of Glendale, and Luke Airbase, west of town just beyond the Haley's farm.[219]

Pearl Harbor changed the tone. No boy from Glendale was lost in the melee, but it didn't take long before bad news was the norm. Alden, in Canada training British pilots on Lockheed high altitude interceptor P-38s, immediately headed back to the United States. He would fly in defense of his country come hell or high water. He went to New Guinea, where he joined the Thirty-fifth Fighter Group under Major General George C. Kenney. Joe was convinced he could keep Junior on the farm with an exemption, but Junior had other ideas after listening to Alden while on leave before heading out. Junior joined the Marines and spent three and one-half years in the Pacific at Munda and Okinawa. Like so many, he came home determined to leave the war behind.[220]

The war unleashed hysteria and prejudice. A state of panic was drummed up by West Coast Civil Defense Councils within days of the attack on Pearl Harbor. Japanese spies and paramilitary groups were reportedly ready to strike all along the Pacific coast and into Arizona.

Joe Haley Jr., 1942. *Courtesy of the author.*

Approximately 120,000 persons of Japanese ancestry lived in the region, with approximately 700 of them in Arizona. Nearly 60 percent were native-born Japanese—Issei adults who were ineligible by United States law for citizenship. That made them "enemy aliens" once Japan bombed Hawaii. Arizona's governor put the state's Civil Defense Coordinating Council on active wartime status and posted guards at public utilities throughout the state.[221]

It didn't take much coaxing for folks to imagine the bombs bursting over Glendale. Three hundred eager men from the Glendale area volunteered for defense service and began training immediately. The Woman's Club converted its meeting place into the city's casualty station, while other civic organizations across the community lined up to raise support for the Red Cross. The Council warned anyone taking civil defense precautions lightly that Phoenix and the surrounding area was an official military "combat zone" under the command of the Western Defense Command. Should the civilian defense program fail, martial law, like that in effect in Hawaii, was a possibility.[222]

The notion of Japanese spies and sabotage gained steam in the early days of the new year, with the federal government's continuing talk of enemy aliens and "Fifth Column" Nazi and Japanese intelligence efforts in the United States. Spy talk brought increased pressure for evacuation of enemy aliens. By mid-February, the president gave the United States military power to prescribe any area as off limits and to evacuate anyone.[223]

Most of Glendale's people of Japanese heritage were gone by the first of June: first to a camp in Mayer, near Prescott, then joining the eighteen thousand others from California at the camp at Poston.[224]

Concerns about food production with Japanese farmers out of the loop proved real enough. Everything was suddenly in short supply. People, encouraged just weeks before to bolster the economy by spending, were suddenly urged, even *ordered*, to conserve and sacrifice. Tires and new cars were some of the first things to go. Quickly converting to defense manufacturing, auto makers and tire manufacturers rolled out "Car Conservation" and "Save Those Tires" campaigns almost as fast as towns like Glendale organized their civil defense. Victor Brooks's Western Auto dealership felt the pinch immediately. The Salt River Valley's largest bank, Valley National, pressed customers to keep deposits in the bank rather than the Depression's coffee can. Greyhound Bus Lines flatly told civilians to forego summer vacation travel and curtail business trips to make room for military personnel. Perhaps the most demanding of all was the government's war rationing program. Beginning with sugar, the government eventually controlled everything from gasoline to shoes, including over two hundred kinds of food.[225]

As in World War I, the military needed grains and beef to feed the troops. The story for cotton was different. Government reserves were high in the early months, resulting in low demand for cotton. Production remained low through the duration of the war.[226]

It didn't take long for farmers of most types of crops to realize they were fighting a war of their own. With the young men gone, remaining men and women took better paying jobs in the factories sprouting up all around the Valley. That left farm labor to the farmers themselves, bringing farming to a near standstill. The United States and Mexico hashed out an agreement for 200,000 braceros to work temporarily in the United States, but contract issues delayed the process. Only 277 braceros finally made it to the Salt River Valley to harvest vegetables and citrus that spring. The Salt River Valley Water Users' Association felt the labor pinch in keeping ditches and canals repaired. Farmers everywhere were desperate for labor. The solution, most farmers agreed, was to get the public and government to give farm production the same priority as manufacturing. Santa Fe Railroad added their support to western farmers' pleas, running ads suggesting people stay off railways and spend their vacations, instead, volunteering on farms, orchards or in canneries.[227]

Labor shortages were nowhere more acute than on Joe and Ollie's farm. Not only was Junior gone, but Cion, too. Joe and Ollie were left with a good seventy acres planted in cotton needing to be chopped, thinned and regularly irrigated on their main farm. Down the road was the ten-acre piece in alfalfa. The twenty acres back on Lateral 22 held Ollie's large one-acre vegetable garden, along with another nineteen acres of alfalfa. On top of all that were the fifteen milk cows, a few calves, chickens, the pig, one mean steer and the repairs that came along daily. There was no help available, from any sector. The two of them did it all.

Things got even worse when Joe got sick with pneumonia in April. Ed and Dowell McAllister helped Ollie with the milking and LouEdna brought dinner most days before she left for work in town, but the burden of the farm those weeks fell entirely on Ollie's strong but weary shoulders. She chopped cotton all day, irrigated many nights and tried to nurse Joe in between the tasks. For his part, Joe was sure he would leave this world soon and needed all of Ollie's attention. Genevieve stepped in to help one Saturday by starting at the wash, but Ollie told her to "drop it and get out of my way." Ollie's well of patience had run dry. After weeks of sickness, Joe finally returned to work and took some of the load off Ollie. The two concluded they couldn't go on and listed the outlying acres for sale, hoping to unload some of the workload quickly.

Junior ended up on the island of Munda, part of a joint-force contingent set to shut down the Japanese effort to build a new airfield after their loss on Guadalcanal. A month of wading in swamps and eating fish heads never left him. The next offensive was Guam, but he didn't get to go. Down to 120 pounds from malaria, Junior shipped out to the hospital in New Zealand. Back at camp, he got word that Alden went down while testing his plane.

Rebecca picked up the phone and called Ollie when they got the news, her voice barely a whisper as Luther shuffled out the back door, walking slowly to the barn, hoping to find a piece of his boy there. Junior was hollow the rest of his life without Alden. The war lost its meaning with the news. He dragged through the rest of its days.

Okinawa cleared up any doubts Junior had about evil and Hell. There, he carried his best buddy, torn to bits, down Sugar Loaf on one of his many crusades up the death-trap mountain. The buddy was the hero, not Junior, he always said, his mouth clinched, every muscle taut. A true Marine, Junior stayed on Okinawa through the clean-up of over 100,000 dead civilians who were used as human shields. Not long after, the war was over and they sent him home—via the United States Navy Hospital in San Diego.

An irrigated field of cotton. *Courtesy of the Library of Congress, Prints & Photographs Division, FSA/OWI collection, lc-dig-fsa-8b31903.*

7

CADILLAC

Junior Haley sat ramrod straight in his seat as the bus made the turn around the White Tank Mountains into the Salt River Valley. After four years and all he'd been through, he was almost home. He sat back suddenly, stunned. Mile after mile of warplanes, parked wing to wing, spread as far as the eye could see. Eyes brimming with tears he hadn't shed in years, Junior didn't know if the sight of the graveyard of planes silenced by peace was beautiful or terrible. Home had changed while he was gone.

Half an hour later, the bus pulled into the station in downtown Phoenix. Joe and Ollie weren't hard to find, their eyes looking to find their boy after a lifetime of worry. Talk was awkward, like a dance between strangers. Walking toward the dusty Hudson, Ollie said, "Everyone is anxious to see you. Rebecca and Luther, especially."

Junior hadn't planned on facing up to the loss. He couldn't imagine why they wanted to see a live boy after losing Alden.

Junior waved his dad off when asked if he wanted to drive. It had been too long. He sat back and watched as they made their slow way up Grand Avenue, stopping at lights at every six points. Packing sheds along the railroad tracks were busy, lettuce was going east this time of year.

He made his sad visit to Rebecca and Luther's a few days later. There he found the dusty barn still waiting, Alden's airplane intact, living longer than the boy.

Junior didn't plan on staying in Glendale beyond his six-week leave. He'd check on things and re-enlist when he reported back. He hoped to make it to the Marine baseball team and get picked up by the majors, if he was lucky. He hadn't counted on the emotional pull of home, or the power of his old nemesis: duty.

His folks looked bad. Ollie was a tired old woman, eyes flat, with the light gone out. "What the hell happened here?" Junior asked himself as he watched her during the first few hours home. Her excitement over his return was subdued, like she didn't have enough energy to greet the son she hadn't seen for nearly four years. The wear and tear on Junior's dad was more expected, though significant. Still, Junior was furious about the sale of two more parcels of land, for almost nothing, while he was gone. There was no help anywhere during the war, the folks told him.[228]

It wasn't long before Junior met up with his old buddies. They wanted him to stay, bargain with his dad for more control on the farm.

"Stay here and prosper," one of the guys argued, "all hell is breaking loose here. The Salt River Valley is boom land, Junior. Soldiers coming home are hungry. Broken down Europe is starving and can't find a plow. We've got the land, the water and the plows. What's more, walk around a day or two and you'll see all kinds of people you don't know. It's crazy. Battle-tired soldiers are everywhere and they are going to keep on coming. They don't want to go back to those rotting cold old towns they came from. This place is going to explode. And those damn Soviets—they're the next big enemy. Mark my words. It's just a matter of time and they'll have Luke back up and running."[229]

"They closed Luke?" Junior asked. "What the hell did they do that for?"

"They're government, Junior. Your employer, buddy, if you are dumb enough to stay in. Haven't you seen how they make decisions?"

"Haven't you had enough war, buddy?" the other friend asked. "You go back in, you aren't going to be playing ball. You will be playing war again. Even if you do go to the pros, those Marines will get you back first sign of hostilities, just you watch. Buddy, smarten up."

Joe thought over what the guys said as he lay on a blanket on a ditch bank irrigating for the next few nights. The economics and thought of getting dragged back into another war were strong points, but what sealed the deal was Helen Brooks's niece, Edith. She was new, different and opinionated.[230]

The case he presented to his folks for a three-way partnership stressed the fact that farming was booming. Farmers garnered higher prices than at any time since 1920. Still, Joe and Ollie met him only half way, agreeing to significantly expand and upgrade the dairy and loan him money for additional cows, a new milking barn and equipment.

Part of their land was another matter. Junior could pour his sweat and labor into their land for however many years it took for them to die. He would get half. His sister would get the other. Junior begrudgingly took the deal, though it infuriated Edith.[231]

Junior's friends overstated the Valley's economic boom in those early days immediately after the war. Plants closed as the government withdrew its military contracts, cancelling leases. Yet, the infrastructure of a new Valley was forming. Local banks reported new loan records at the close of 1945, mostly to small businesses. Agriculture stayed strong, though farmers were still begging for labor. Reclamation officials predicted a statewide increase in population by twenty-five thousand in the next five years.[232]

Government kept tight reins on the economy in those early days after the war in an attempt to control inflation and avoid the hardship that sent everyone reeling after World War I. But it didn't take long to realize this postwar was different than the last. Laborers called a strike in the steel industry, leading International Harvester to tell farmers that any kind of settlement would mean high prices passed on to farmers.[233]

There was no illusion of peace. The Soviet Union was the next enemy, grabbing what it could of devastated Europe. The bomb upped the ante. Growing insecurity made the United States government cautious, holding onto stockpiles and controls, particularly on commodities such as cotton.[234]

The flood of servicemen and women returning home pressed against government's tight hand, creating its own economy. Yielding to the pressure, government lifted price controls in 1946, unleashing a flood of pent-up consumer want. Auto manufactures worked nonstop to retool but could not begin to meet demand.[235]

Baseball joined the migration west. Spring training finally came to the Valley in 1947 with the Cleveland Indians and the New York Giants. Seizing the day, the Santa Fe Trailways bus line advertised for people to take their first post-war vacations. Junior Haley rode east to muster out of the Marines for good, abandoning his dream of playing ball with the pros. He returned to marry Edith in the fall of 1946 in a small ceremony in Victor and Helen's living room. The young couple returned from a brief honeymoon in California to live in town with Edith's mother.[236]

Junior poured himself into clearing land and building the new cow barn, complete with a large cold storage locker, concrete flooring with drainage ditches and ten stalls to handle automatic milking machines. Outside the barn he constructed corrals for wet and dry cows as well as calves. He cleared a narrow lane down the far north boundary of the property to access the corrals for feeding, as well as the back fields. With the barn completed, he and Joe looked for stock. They soon raised the size of their herd to forty and got clearance to sell Grade A milk. The new procedures for ensuring sterile milk were confusing, but no one grumbled for long as money for the Grade A milk poured in. Their move to upgrade was right in step with the times. Statewide, dairymen produced over 135,000 tons of Grade A milk, raising dairy's overall percentage of agricultural income by 3 percentage points in one year.[237]

Junior's return to the farm changed the pattern of Ollie's days. She still rose before five o'clock to line the wet cows up, slapping the hinds and yelling to get them in line while the men got the machines going. Once the first line advanced, Ollie hurried inside to help wash down udders before Joe and Junior connected the milking machines. Once done, she headed outside to repeat the process. As the last cows passed into the barn, she turned to feeding the young calves recently separated from their mothers. Her work with milking finished, Ollie hurried back to the house to fix breakfast while the two men cleaned the machinery, stored the milk and washed down the barn. They repeated the whole process again in midafternoon every day of the week.

The difference came after breakfast. Now Ollie had time to attend Women's Missionary Union, visit with friends or just clean her house before afternoon milking. Her laundry hung blazing white on the line every Monday like it did before the war. She got a permanent wave at the beauty parlor, a new dress and shoes for church or ran into town to pick up something at the newly opened supermarket. Then her papa took sick and died, bringing everyone except Fannie and Marguritte, who lived in far off states, home.

Ollie's role and identity changed in early 1948 with the birth of Junior's first child, a girl. Genevieve followed a year and a half later with a boy. Not long after, Ollie begged out of milking duty for a week to care for Junior's girl while Edith gave birth to a second girl. By then, Ollie was often seen walking the fields with a toddler in tow. Joe softened with the children, taking them with him to the chicken coop, grape arbor or for a ride in the high old swing Willie hung in the yard years before for other children.

Agricultural income more than doubled from 1947 to 1952. Approximately 43 percent of that was income from cotton. Postwar demands for wheat and other food for starving Europe supported a 50 percent expansion in acreage. Cotton claimed half of all agricultural acreage statewide, 39 percent picked by mechanical pickers. Goodyear Farms celebrated fifty years of success in 1952, reminding cotton farmers of its contributions to cotton farming and crop rotation methods. As farmers pushed cotton production further, water supplies stretched thinner. Drought during the last decade, along with expansion, pushed supply to the limit. Most irrigation was pumped water.[238]

Dependence on irrigation didn't blind farmers to the vagaries of nature. Rain was still temperamental. In 1951, it stayed away for months and then unleashed its fury in August, filling rivers and streams.[239]

Local Japanese farmers, returned from relocation camps, found a niche market in flowers, as well as traditional crops. Over two hundred first-generation Japanese Americans in the Glendale area were finally eligible for citizenship under the McCarran Omnibus Immigration and Naturalization Bill of 1952.[240]

Farmers' workload eased when Congress passed legislation establishing a permanent bracero program, bringing in farm laborers from Mexico. The vast majority of workers in Arizona and California were used in some point of cotton production. Junior qualified, hiring Jesus and settling him and his family in a small shack on the southeast corner of the farm. Jesus picked up most of the irrigating duties, quickly earning Joe's respect. In 1949, Arizona cotton production hit half of one million bales for the first time, prompting the pointless old warnings for farmers to hold back, not go "cotton crazy."[241]

A ditch with earthen sides. Shacks were typically used to house temporary workers, n.d. This scene was typical into the 1950s. *Courtesy of the Glendale Arizona Historical Society.*

Hired help eased the load, even in the milk barn, as Joe, Ollie and Junior increased their herd significantly. Junior had time to play baseball and socialize. He and Edith joined the 20/30 Club, a social service group. It kept them in a social whirl for some time, partying with old friends and meeting new people just moved to the Valley. Glendale's organizations were busy in these prosperous times. While the Woman's Club focused on welfare, several men's organizations staged large events. The Lion's Club held a rodeo, complete with parade, Kiwanis put on a Salad Bowl parade and football game. The American Institute of Foreign Trade, occupying former Thunderbird Field, hosted a Latin American "neighbors" fiesta with cooperation from the Glendale Chamber of Commerce. The event attracting the largest crowd was the annual Fiesta of the Junta Patriotica. The dance, food and parade always pulled a mixed crowd.[242]

That integration went only so far. In early 1952, parents of two students at the town's predominantly Mexican American elementary school sued for an injunction to end segregation in Glendale schools. The school district lifted mandatory segregation, giving spots to Mexican American students at the other school when vacancies arose; but given the overcrowding, the move was mostly a gesture until the new school, which was under construction, was completed.[243]

Junior was right when he observed home had changed, but it was a toss up whether it was home or Junior himself who had changed the most. His and Edith's lifestyle was a breech in the eyes of Joe and Ollie. For generations, on all sides of the family, the church was the center of family social life. Even Jack Brooks gave it a certain respect. But Junior would have none of it after the war. Edith and her mother took the children to the Methodist Church, but Junior showed up only to see the children perform. Clubs, baseball and close friends replaced the social role of church for the young couple.

There was change in the family, too. Alden's death and the war took the spirit out of the Brooks family. Gone were the days when everyone gathered after church for tamale pie, a freezer of ice cream and a little catching up. Rebecca hosted an old-fashioned Brooks Easter Sunday dinner in 1953 to celebrate the return of her youngest daughter and her military husband from a long stint in Europe. Forty-three, including several of Fannie's grown daughters, gathered on Rebecca's manicured lawn. Fannie and Leo still lived in Missouri. Marguritte and Ham now ran a ranch in Texas.

The biggest changes came in the economy. The Korean War finished what World War II started, rejuvenating manufacturing and technology,

AT-6 planes at the Luke Air Force Base, west of Glendale, n.d. *Courtesy of the Glendale Arizona Historical Society.*

setting it on a course to transform the Valley. Most critical were the return of AiResearch, reactivation of Luke Air Force Base and arrival of a new player: Motorola. It wasn't long before jets flew over the farm daily, pilots and other personnel racing down Lateral 21 on their way to the base. Reynolds Aluminum, new owner of the Alcoa plant west of Phoenix, operated at full swing, supplying products for military aircraft. Motorola opened a plant east of Phoenix. Dozens of smaller companies provided support for larger manufacturing.[244]

Farming held its own as the Valley economy began its transformation. Cotton, lettuce, melons, grains and dairy all reaped the benefit of high demand during tense Cold War days. But signs of future shift were there. A regional grocery chain began, in 1953, to haul milk in from California, inciting local dairymen. Edith joined other dairy wives on the picket line.

Few reflected on the fact that high farm productivity in the Valley borrowed water from the future. Most of the water flowing in the Haley's ditches in the 1950s came from underground, not from mountain rivers and reservoirs central to the original reclamation plan. The last good runoff was back in 1940–41. By the end of 1948, that water was insufficient, forcing pumping and a further drop in the water table.[245]

Approving the compact in 1944, Arizona turned its energy to gaining approval and funding for a system to deliver Colorado River water to the heart of the state where it was needed most. Called the "Central Arizona Project," the plan called for a 336-mile aqueduct from Lake Havasu to bring one 1.2 million acre-feet to Phoenix and Tucson. The proposal was perpetually rebuffed in Congress, primarily because issues with California stood in the way. Calling it a "crisis for our state," Arizona appealed again to the Supreme Court in 1952 to settle the differences. This time the Court took the case.[246]

Meanwhile, the Salt River Valley Water Users' Association was reinventing itself. Postwar urban growth, coupled with the fast acceptance of air conditioning, strained electric power resources. Instigator of growth or savvy trend reader, the association believed its analysts, who said the Valley would be 90 percent urban by 2000. In 1952, Water Users' made the decisive move into the urban market, contracting to provide the City of Phoenix with domestic water. Other cities quickly jumped on board. In addition, the association began delivering electricity from Hoover Dam to Valley residents. It focused on conservation efforts for farmers, lining ditches and canals as it threw its increasing weight into lobbying efforts for the Central Arizona Project.[247]

Junior wanted to expand. Farmers all around were making money hand over fist on cotton. Wanting his own piece of the action, Junior ratcheted up his campaign, practicing a little "divide and conquer" on Joe and Ollie. He somehow convinced Joe to go shopping for land. Both knew how much Ollie wanted a new house, so they wanted to be sure the land had a good house on it before approaching her.

"Hell no. And that is my final answer," Ollie shouted before she slammed out of the kitchen the morning Junior brought up the idea.

"She didn't even give me a chance!" Junior complained as the screen door banged.

"Oh, she's got that bee in her bonnet about a house. You know how she is when she gets riled up about something. Wait 'til she cools down. That is one stubborn woman," Joe put in.

Anxious to move on a deal he thought would not hold long, Junior approached his mom again a little while later.

"Please, Mama, just go and see this house. It's real nice. A lot bigger than what you have now. I'll paint it all for you myself."

"Look, Junior. You need to understand something. I am not moving into some house that smells of a thousand breakfasts from some other folks. All the paint in China will not take away that old breakfast smell in a house. I have waited this long, put up this long and I am having a brand spanking new house or no house at all and no one is using any money to buy any more land until I get that house. Period. You understand? So you and your dad can just rid yourselves of your notion about more land with some old house for Mama on it. It ain't gonna happen."

What Ollie did not say was that if Junior and Edith could buy a brand new three-bedroom house, so could she.

With a third child on the way, it had been obvious to everyone a year or so earlier that Junior and Edith needed more space. Joe had an old house picked out and was about ready to sign the contract to have it moved onto the farm when Edith got wind of the plan. All the pent-up anger of the past six years came spewing out. She let him know she thought he had some unfettered gall to think he could just go pick out some old house for her. But that wasn't the half of it. Edith informed Joe she was never living on that damn farm under his spying, judgmental eye. Not now, not ever.

Junior and Edith's new house wasn't that grand. One of twenty in a small development teeming with children just outside the Glendale city limits, it was built on a dead-end dirt road, backed up to a dairy and lacked city sewer. Despite the lack of niceties, the houses sold long before they were built.

Returning home from the war, thousands of servicemen and women turned west, landing in California and Arizona. Passing through the region during the war, they determined then to return to be part of the dynamic optimism they saw and liked. Ready to live on their own terms, they came back to the West in droves. They were pushy about getting roofs over their heads. An estimated 2,500 newcomers a year moved into the Phoenix area between 1950 and 1960, gobbling up houses as fast as builders could get them up. John F. Long was just one of many young builders throwing their hats into the housing ring. Long started out with the intention of building only a handful. Demand was so high, he built 1,600 before 1954, when he began "Maryvale," a development of over 35,000 homes in the West Valley.

Other builders launched developments throughout the Valley as Federal Housing Administration and Veterans Administration financing made home-buying accessible for veterans and other middle class and lower middle class wage earners. Houses were typically three bedrooms, one or two baths and masonry construction, with a single auto carport. Many could be purchased with nothing down. Developments hopscotched over and around farmland, as builders picked the cheapest land, frequently without city services or adequate schools.

Late in 1952, Sam Hoffman announced the start of a development of 1,500 homes just east of John F. Long's development. Some in Glendale wished Hoffman would move his development in the direction of their town. Others breathed a sigh of relief when he didn't. Approximately 1,500 homes were just what they did not need, they argued. As early as 1951, Glendale's pro and con development camps began taking their positions. At the heart of the debate lay the question of annexation.[248]

The Glendale Chamber of Commerce led the proponents of annexation. Lack of adequate housing was a "bottleneck" to progress, the chamber declared in December 1951. Houses brought more people to Glendale businesses, they said, and increased the tax base. As importantly, the town of eight thousand needed development and annexation to maintain its identity and stave off being gobbled up by Phoenix like the small agricultural towns around Los Angeles. In another ten years, those nine miles and more would be either part of Glendale or Phoenix. Glendale was out of time. It was do or die.[249]

The city council took the conservative position. New developments needed services: sewer, water and streets, at the least. Early in 1952, the council released an analysis showing little increase in tax revenue from newly annexed fringes in return for such services, leading the council to scale back annexation plans.

The pressures were too great for anyone to hold the conservative stance for long. In 1953, the National Association of Manufacturers predicted Arizona needed an additional thirty-seven thousand single-family homes, valued at over $344 million, by 1960. Construction spending in Glendale doubled in 1952 to $1.5 million, lining the city coffers and easing some council worries. New homes or old, people found some kind of housing around Glendale, flooding the two elementary schools and one high school with children until the high school finally had to adopt double sessions. The influx strained the city's water system, requiring an additional deep well. The message was clear. The town would grow, with or without control. The Glendale City Council established new zoning and planning commissions in response. The town's newspaper chronicled it all, noting: "Rural Glendale is becoming residential." Despite the influx, Glendale's voters affirmed the town's covenant prohibiting sale of liquor.[250]

Like a lot of farmers around, Joe, Ollie and Junior didn't have time for, or interest in, annexation debates at the rotary club, city council or chamber of commerce. The only one remotely interested was Ollie, and what she cared about was all the women getting new houses except her.

Victor and Helen decided to add on to their home in town instead of buying a new home. Victor's Western Auto dealerships were doing well. While the war put him out of the auto dealership business, he still loved new cars, trading for a new one every year. A couple of times he and Helen drove back to Detroit to pick up their new Pontiac.

When Genevieve gave birth to a girl, she and her husband, Ken, bought a small tract home six miles east of the farm. Not long after, Joe and Edith had their first boy, followed a year later by another son. Ollie was now the grandmother of six. She often kept one or two, relieving the busy mothers.

Rebecca knew how much Ollie wanted a new house, so it's doubtful she flaunted the fact that she and Luther were getting out of farming and thinking about building a luxury home in a new section of Glendale. Gradually, they'd sold Alden's things, though everyone said Luther was never the same. By the time Rebecca moved, Ollie was resolved. Her new house was on the drawing board. The house would have a number of extra features including refrigerated air conditioning, a big pantry and a large picture window looking out onto the road. The old house would shelter someone hired to do most of the milking.

After thirty years, LouEdna McAllister still lived in her in-laws' home, waiting for the day that she would have the house of her dreams. She would settle for nothing less. Planning for her own home someday, LouEdna was a fountain of decorating ideas, eager to help Ollie with her new house. Together they chose all new furniture, carpeting and draperies for the large living and dining room. Her house complete, Ollie bought a new dress, new shoes and went to town to get a permanent wave. She was ready to host the Women's Missionary Union for farmwomen and merchants' wives alike.

Thwarted in his plan to buy land, Junior found a couple of plots to rent for cotton. Once again, Arizona cotton was a player on the international stage. This time, the diplomatic moves worked in favor of United States cotton when Egypt pulled its cotton out of the United States market in order to fulfill its new obligations to Iron Curtain countries. While demand drove farmers like Joe to plant more acreage, advances in yield and increasing mechanization went part of the distance in countering the drain on water supply.[251]

Moving equipment to several locations was awkward, but profits good. With Ollie's house hunger satisfied, Junior began looking again. What he found was a significant rise in land prices.

Aerospace continued to fuel the Valley economy, stimulating a growing service industry and trades supporting the still-booming housing market, like John F. Long's expanding Maryvale. Junior and Edith bought a large four bedroom, three bathroom John Long home on a curving street. Junior immediately had refrigerated air conditioning put in the home. While public buildings had the upgrade, most suburban homes came equipped with only evaporative coolers.

Junior had farther to commute to the farm after the move, but his family almost doubled its living space. Neighbors in the development were generally new to Arizona, coming from all over the country. Many worked at Luke Air Force Base. Most were well educated. There were Mormons, Catholics, Methodists, Baptists, Lutherans and some with no religious ties. Despite the diversity in background, there were few racial differences. Unprepared for the influx, elementary schools were on double session for a couple of years. High school students traveled six miles by city bus before the new high school was built five years later.

The area was unincorporated. Glendale didn't want it. Phoenix hadn't jumped at the chance. That left Maryvale residents contracting with a private rural fire company. Farm plots with open, weed-lined irrigation ditches framed neighborhoods. The single shopping center saw a lot of traffic until Long constructed a competing concern across the street. A small community center and public pool were the center of everything, especially for kids. The school and few churches were the center of culture. Still, demand continued as Long built. In 1959, the need for water and sewer pushed Glendale and Phoenix to negotiate contiguous boundaries. Phoenix succeeded in annexing one area further east. When Glendale annexed another in 1961, it doubled the city's size.[252]

Ollie made the drive to Junior's new place several times a week in her second Ford. Driving it back to Missouri a few times, she'd proven the Ford could speed through little towns as well as the best of them, but the car didn't win any points with her doing it. Every Sunday, Joe pulled in front of the church next to Victor's new Pontiac on one side and a new Cadillac on the other. Half the time Victor got out of his car, walked around and then asked Joe when he was going to part with some of that money in the bank and put Ollie in a decent ride. Joe would just laugh. Ollie would slam the door of the dirty Ford, straighten her shoulders and try to act like not a thing was bothering her as she climbed the steps of the church.

Ollie, Joe and Junior were so busy taking care of the farm, not one of them had noticed the changes going on around them: the seismic shift in values and power. The old state mantra "copper, cotton and cattle" was reduced to one word: "GROWTH." Young men from somewhere else ruled now: overnight millionaires, many in housing and land speculation.[253]

"Rural Glendale is becoming residential" foretold more than most people wanted to consider at the time. Early on, changes around Glendale looked benign. Farmers selling out to developers in 1953 and 1954 did so voluntarily, often retiring or relocating further out. As new neighborhoods spread, however, the tone changed. Clashes with existing farms increased. Farmers created dust, sprayed chemicals and often owned smelly cows with mounds of fly-attracting manure. New populations needed water for their lawns, trees, cooking and drinking. Developers began buying orchards for the water rights, leaving the trees to die slow, thirsty deaths. In a flash, developers paved over some of the best agricultural soil in the world. The agricultural footprint of the Valley was on its way to becoming history.

Joe and Ollie never would have thought Luke Air Force Base would end up playing villain in their own story. All of those fresh-faced boys lined the avenue during the war, friendly boys like Junior and Alden. Now, Luke was the big employer in the West Valley. Commissioned personnel usually found housing in one of the new subdivisions dotting the West Valley landscape, but enlisted personnel had more of a challenge finding something affordable. Trailer parks were the perfect solution.

Junior, Joe and Ollie woke up to the wheels of progress when someone submitted plans for a trailer park to back up into their cow corral. Rushing to the planning and zoning meeting, the trio realized that the Glendale they knew had disappeared while they were busy expanding the farm. They had no friends in city hall. They didn't know any of these people in planning and zoning. The trailer park was approved. The Haley farm was the underdog from that point on.

No dairy farm survives long in a neighborhood, no matter how long it has been there first. The trailer park brought dozens of neighbors who did not like the smell of manure or the presence of flies. It wasn't long before the milk inspector was a weekly visitor, riding Junior about his manure pile and the condition of his corrals and threatening fines. It was a miracle Junior didn't land in jail. He knew it was only a matter of time before the inspector shut him down.[254]

None of it turned out the way Junior planned. The Valley's big boom went a different direction—away from him. Ten years older, too old for baseball, all he knew was farming. He looked at land further out, but prices were too high. There was no choice but to close down the dairy.

The day they loaded the cows to be shipped off felt like someone had died. As the last truck rolled out in early evening, Ollie looked at the empty corrals in the softening light. Tears streaming down her cheeks, she walked on through the milk barn. The emptiness seemed hollow, not right. Ollie had no solution. Her time was over.

The auction was gut-wrenching for Junior. To watch the auctioneer sell equipment he'd mortgaged his soul for spelled failure, pure and simple.

It was always about the land for Joe. He'd come close to losing it more than once, his very soul on the line. No one, not even Ollie, really understood that.

Nothing else could tear his guts out after the agony of exhaustion, worry and self-doubt of those young cotton days. Tired of milking, tired of farming, Joe saddled up his horse, Tumbleweed, and surveyed what mattered to him. Let a developer come and try to buy it off of him. He'd give the man thirty seconds to get off his property.

Junior gone, Joe rented out the fields. Watching another man's tractor in the fields made Ollie restless. With money in the bank from their half of the cow sale, she decided the time was right to go to church in style. One day, she and Joe drove to Phoenix early, headed for the Cadillac dealership. They left a few hours later, driving a 1960 four-door hardtop Deville that was longer than a city block. Joe drove it once in awhile, but everyone knew the car was Ollie's. She washed it most every Saturday afternoon and pulled in right next to her brother Victor in front of church the next morning. Then Victor went to Detroit, brought back another new car, and the glitter was gone out of pulling up in front of church in the Cadillac. Ollie could hit one hundred miles per hour in that thing and not even know it. She proved it more than once driving to Missouri. But, like most things in life, Ollie learned, the Cadillac got a few dings and lost its luster. After that, it wasn't much different from the Ford.

It took forty years, but Arizona won the war for water. In 1964, the Supreme Court decided that Arizona should receive the 2.8 million acre-feet plus water from its tributaries. In addition, the Court established water rights for Native Americans along the Colorado River and spelled out states' rights versus federal government issues. Arizona's congressional delegation succeeded in pushing through the Central Arizona Project not long after.[255]

After following the news about the river fight for forty years, both Joe and Ollie were glad to be on the winning side. They both knew their land would probably never see a drop of the water. Joe rode Tumbleweed around the place until he was well into his nineties and the horse was so old that she could barely carry the frail man. He died in 1981, at ninety-three, setting in motion the process of selling the farm. Ollie immediately moved to town. She no longer felt safe on the farm after hoodlums tied up and robbed both her and Joe. Though the perpetrators were not caught, sheriff deputies told Ollie it was likely she and Joe were being watched from the trailer park. Junior and Edith moved to the farm to keep a presence there until the land sale was completed, Junior thwarting one major robbery attempt in the meantime. They built a nice home north of town and travelled some with proceeds of the land sale.

Ollie traded in the Cadillac for an Oldsmobile and bought a nice doublewide mobile home in the retirement community where Helen and Marguritte lived. Rebecca and Leolia lived within a couple of miles. Genevieve, a recent widow, was close by. Ollie had a great time for a brief while. One day, she received a call from her cousin Nannie, Margaret Brooks's girl. In the course of conversation, the cousin mentioned she'd just gotten a new Cadillac.

Ollie replied, "Oh, I guess I've had mine."

Epilogue

Joe Haley Jr. (Junior) inched out of the car, his back stiff, legs cramped. War and years of sitting on a tractor had caught up with him, taking their toll, numbering his days. He'd spent the better part of this day with his daughter and her young grandson, Josh, visiting the landmarks of Junior's past. It was the daughter's idea, this "history day," designed to give the boy a sense of his heritage before Junior was gone or no longer lucid. They hit the old church, schools, ball fields and even his favorite coffee shop. They left off the cemetery by some unspoken agreement between Junior and the daughter, despite the fact that Edith and almost everyone else that really mattered to him were already there.

This was the last stop, this sea of look-alike houses lined up on narrow streets running east to west. Junior used to turn his tractor around down there at the end of the street he now faced. He'd swing the machinery wide, heading back the other direction in a monotonous rhythm he repeated a million times over. A big, lush tree stood at the back edge of the field then, drinking all it wanted from the ditches that intersected at the far corner. More than once, he blessed that tree as he climbed down off the tractor, sweat rolling the dust off his face faster than he could wipe it. Maybe that tree saved his life once or twice. Felt like it anyway. The tree went the way of progress, he could see.

Memory took over as Junior stood there, painting a canvas more real than the one right before his eyes. "Look, Josh," Junior motioned, his arm outstretched. "The old house stood right there, big tall trees all around to cool it down years before any air conditioning. Brought our beds into the yard and slept out of doors in the summer. Over there, behind the house was the chicken coop and the pen for the steers we used to fatten. All this," he said, sweeping both arms, "was the work yard and the hay barn. Out there were the fields."

"What's that over there?" the boy questioned, pointing south.

"What do you mean?" Junior asked, suddenly jarred back from the past.

"Oh, that's the big football stadium," the daughter quickly answered, knowing it to be a sore spot for her dad.

"Hey Dad," she continued, "LouEdna's place looks pretty good. I wonder what they will do with it now that she's gone."

"Oh, I don't know. Funny to see it with a traffic signal on the corner," Junior answered.

The three returned to the car and drove the short distance to what was the northeast corner of the old farm. Getting out again, Junior described the former milk barn to Josh and how the cow corrals stretched west behind it.

"I cleared the way for this street here so I could drive my tractor back to feed the cows and work in the fields in the back forty," Junior explained. "Wasn't paved then, of course. Your grandma was the principal user of the drive, though, her and that horse of hers, Tumbleweed. Ever hear of that horse, Josh?"

"Yeah, Grandma tells us stories all the time about Tumbleweed. I wish I could have rode her."

"Sure was a good horse," Junior reflected, walking toward the car. He stopped suddenly, eyeing a short length of old ditch on a corner between the former farm property and neighboring land. Squatting on painful legs, he began to explain to Josh the concept of irrigation: dams, canals, the mechanics of gravity flow, how the farmer receives water for crops. Rising slowly, Junior continued, describing how the ancient Indians first built an elaborate irrigation system, then disappeared, perhaps because of drought. Later, Junior said, white men built big dams in the mountains to conserve the water and snow runoff until it was needed. It wasn't long, however, Junior continued, before people in the Valley needed more and began to pump water from the underground rivers, depleting them faster than nature could replenish the supply.

"Josh," the old man said taking a fistful of soil in his hand, sifting it through his fingers. "This is some of the best soil in the world, but it isn't worth a plug nickel without water. Water is the gold of the desert. It's the boss, not men. Get that turned around and you will all be the losers."

Notes

Chapter 1

1. *Arizona Gazette* (Phoenix, AZ), February 17, 1900, 8; March 6, 1900, 6; September 1, 1900 ,1; January 30, 1901, 6; September 22, 1901, 1.
2. Ibid., July 13, 1899, 1; August 10, 1899, 5.
3. Ibid., May 19, 1899, 8; January 13, 1900, 8; January 20, 1900, 8; August 9, 1900, 8; December 21, 1900, 8.
4. See discussion of the Panic of 1893 in: Allan Nevins, Henry Steele Commager and Jeffrey Morris, *Pocket History of the United States* (New York: Simon and Schuster, 1992).
5. Robert E. Kravetz and Alex Jay Kimmelman, *Healthseekers in Arizona* (Phoenix: Academy of Medical Sciences of the Maricopa Medical Society, 1998).
6. Bureau of the Census, "Schedule No. 1-Population," Township 2N, Range 2E, in *Arizona Decennial Census Population in Retrospect* (Maricopa County, AZ, 1900), 13.
7. Earl A. Zarbin, *Roosevelt Dam: A History to 1911* (Phoenix: Salt River Project, 1984), 19–29.
8. *Arizona Gazette*, June 4, 1899; Geoffrey P. Mawn, "Phoenix, Arizona: Central City of the Southwest, 1870–1920," Dissertation (Arizona State University, 1979), 219, 226–227; Carol J. Coffelt St. Clair and Charles S. St. Clair, *Glendale: Images of America* (Charleston, SC: Arcadia Publishing, 2006), 9.

9. *Arizona Gazette*, April 29, 1903, 3; May 9, 1903, 5; Jared Smith, *Making Water Flow Uphill: The History of Agriculture in Mesa, Arizona* (Mesa, AZ: Mesa Historical Museum, 2004).

10. *Arizona Gazette*, October 19, 1900, 1.

11. Cartwright School District No. 83, "100 Years of Quality Education, 1884–1984," Centennial Program, Cartwright School District (Phoenix, AZ, 1984); Territory of Arizona, "Report of the Superintendent of Public Instruction, 1898–1900" (Phoenix: Arizona State Archives); *Arizona Gazette*, January 27, 1900.

12. *Arizona Gazette*, January 27, 1900, 5.

13. Ibid., January 13, 1900, 8, 20, 27; February 10, 1900, 5; August 9, 1900, 8–9.

14. Pearl B. Cramm to M.B. Brooks, *Warranty Deed*, Territory of Arizona, Deed book, 56.

15. Photo of Opera House (Phoenix: Arizona State Archives, n.d.); Zarbin, *Roosevelt Dam*, 29–40.

16. *Arizona Gazette*, September 1, 1900, 1.

17. Karen L. Smith, *The Magnificent Experiment: Building the Salt River Reclamation Project, 1890–1917* (Tucson: University of Arizona Press, 1986).

18. *Arizona Gazette*, October 17, 1901, 1; October 19, 1901, 1; May 16, 1902, 8.

19. Ibid., July 6, 1902, 1, 5; July 23, 1902, 5; August 5, 1902, 5.

20. Zarbin, *Roosevelt Dam*, 38.

21. *Arizona Gazette*, October 3, 1902, 1; Zarbin, *Roosevelt Dam*, 46–84.

22. *Arizona Gazette*, February 6, 1903, 5; March 14, 1903, 1.

23. Kathleen Noon, "Industry Came to Glendale: Sugar Beet Factory History, Glendale, AZ: 1903–1910," http://www.molokane.org/molokan/Locations/Americas/Arizona/Noon.htm.

24. *Arizona Gazette*, April 14, 1904, 3; July 10, 1904, 3; July 11, 1904, 8.

25. Ibid., July 22, 1904, 1; July 23, 1904, 8; Zarbin, *Roosevelt Dam*, 91–92.

26. *Arizona Gazette*, August 7, 1907; Appropriators Canal Company, *Articles of Incorporation*, Arizona State Archives, 1905.

27. *Arizona Gazette*, August 24, 1904, 1; October 5, 1904, 1.

28. Zarbin, *Roosevelt Dam*, 103–107.

29. Ibid., 107.

30. *Arizona Gazette*, March 30, 1905, 8; June 15, 1905, 1; June 21, 1905, 8.

31. *Arizona Gazette*, January 28, 1907, 4; Earl A. Zarbin, *Salt River Project: Four Steps Forward: 1902–1920* (Phoenix: Salt River Project, 1995), 3–32.

32. *Arizona Gazette*, April 8, 1907, 1; July 16, 1907, 5.

Chapter 2

33. *Arizona Gazette,* January 3, 1907, 2; January 31, 1907, 1.

34. Ada Fern (née Bobbe) Goodman, Interviews by the author, Tape recording (Glendale, AZ): January 9, 2001; January 24, 2001; April 13, 2002.

35. *Arizona Gazette,* September 14, 1901; September 17, 1903, 5; August 1904, 8; Harry David Ware, "Alcohol, Temperance and Prohibition in Arizona," Dissertation (Arizona State University, 1995), 148; Robert L. Griswold, "Anglo Women and Domestic Ideology in the American West in the Nineteenth and Early Twentieth Centuries," in *Western Women: Their Land, Their Lives,* edited by Lillian Schlissel, Vicki L. Ruiz and Janice Monk (Albuquerque: University of New Mexico Press, 1988), 15–34.

36. Irene Cartwright, Holmes "History of the Cartwright Family," Notes (Phoenix Public Library, 1993).

37. *Arizona Gazette,* January 16, 1899; February 6, 1901, 2; June 26, 1901, 2; February 6, 1902, 8; George M. Marsden, *Fundamentalism and American Culture: The Shaping of Twentieth-Century Evangelism, 1870–1925* (New York: Oxford University Press, 1980), 6, 32–39.

38. *Arizona Gazette,* March 6, 1907, 8; March 14, 1907, 4; March 15, 1907, 6; March 16, 1907, 3.

39. Ibid., July 9, 1903, 2; July 1, 1905, 8.

40. Donald P. Hustad, *Jubilate! Church Music in the Evangelical Tradition* (Carol Stream, IL: Hope Publishing Company, 1981), 151; Robert J. Morgan, *Then Sings My Soul: 150 of the World's Greatest Hymn Stories* (Nashville: Thomas Nelson Press, 2003), 261.

41. *Arizona Gazette,* September 18, 1902, 5; November 2, 1902, 2; October 11, 1903, 6; March 6, 1907, 8; March 11, 1907, 3; March 14, 1907, 4; March 15, 1907, 11; March 16, 1907, 3; March 21, 1907, 7; March 22, 1907, 6; March 25, 1907, 8; March 26, 1907, 4; March 27, 1907, 6; March 29, 1907, 7; March 30, 1907, 3; April 1, 1907, 6; Frank M. Barrios, *Mexicans in Phoenix* (Charleston, SC: Arcadia Publishing, 2008), 7; Matthew C. Whitaker, "In Search of Black Phoenicians: African American Culture and Community in Phoenix, Arizona, 1868–1940," Thesis (Arizona State University, 1997), 28.

42. *Arizona Gazette*, July 24, 1905, 8; March 1907, 8; "Cartwright Methodist Episcopal Church, South." Duplicated history, n.d., Author's collection; James Bykirt says Methodists "enjoyed the greatest success [of denominations]…in Arizona in the late nineteenth century." James Byrkit, "The Word on the Frontier: Anglo Protestant Churches in Arizona 1859–1899," *Journal of Arizona History*, 21 (1980) 78.

43. *Arizona Gazette*, April 1, 1900, 8; April 14, 1900, 8; May 1, 1901, 1.

44. Ibid., May 26, 1901, 2; December 6, 1904, 1; April 28, 1905, 8; February 5, 1906, 8; November 23, 1906, 8; Ware, "Alcohol, Temperance," 158.

45. *Arizona Gazette*, January 20, 1903, 3; April 18, 1906, 1; July 24, 1906, 4; May 2, 1907, 4.

46. Ibid., September 22, 1906, 5; August 12, 1907, 5; December 6, 1907, 4.

47. Ibid., March 8, 1904, 5; April 15, 1907, 5; Whitaker, "In Search," 28.

48. *Arizona Republic* (Phoenix, AZ), July 27, 1901, 2; July 28, 1; Gai Ingham Berlage, *Women in Baseball: The Forgotten History* (Westport, CT: Praeger, 1994), 37.

49. *Arizona Gazette*, October 8, 1906, 4.

50. Ibid., February 14, 1907, 5.

51. Ibid., April 18, 1907, 7.

52. Ibid., June 22, 1907, 5; June 24, 1907, 3; July 5, 1907, 6; September 7, 1907, 6; December 6, 1907, 4.

53. *Glendale News*, October 18, 1912, special edition; Geoffrey Mawn says investors' pulled out of the Arizona Improvement Company, which founded Glendale in 1888, on learning irrigation resources for the plan were inadequate without water storage. The action forced the company to reorganize as the Arizona Water company. Mawn, "Phoenix, Arizona," 225.

54. St. Clair, *Glendale*, 9–24.

55. Noon, "Industry," 6–7.

56. Thomas E. Sheridan, *Arizona: A History* (Tucson: University of Arizona Press, 1995), 210–11.

57. Sandy Finerman, "A History of Glendale Union High District," Manuscript (Phoenix Public Library, 1978).

58. Joe Haley Jr., Interviews with the author, Tape recording (Glendale, AZ): February 28, 2000; March 20, 2000; April 17, 2000; April 28, 2000; July 12, 2000.

59. *Glendale News*, October 11, 1912, 4; January 24, 1913; December 18, 1914; First United Methodist Church of Glendale, Arizona, "A Century in Mission and Ministry," Manuscript, 1994.

60. *Glendale News*, February 1917, Anniversary Edition, 13; Esta Portnoy, "The Russian Molokans: Glendale's Spirited Immigrants," 1981. http:// molokane.org/molokan/Locations/Americas/Arizona/Portnoy/.

61. Sheridan, *Arizona*, 211–12.

62. *Glendale News*, April 9, 1914, 1.

63. Goodman, Interviews.

64. *Glendale News*, February 19, 1915, 1; Goodman, Interviews.

65. First Baptist Church, Glendale, "History of First Baptist Church of Glendale, Arizona, 1906–1980," Church files; "1985 Marks Seventy-Nine Years of Fruitful Ministry for First Baptist Church of Glendale Organized March 23, 1906," Church files, circa 1985.

66. Postcard, Minnie Scholl to Nannie Haley, March 1915, Copy, Author's collection.

67. *Glendale News*, March 5, 1915, 1.

Chapter 3

68. Haley, Interviews.

69. Ibid.

70. *Glendale News*, April 1916.

71. *Glendale News*, January 11, 1918; January 8, 1918.

72. Ibid., March 5, 1915, 1.

73. Ibid., January 5, 1917, 1; October 10,1917, 2; Sheridan, *Arizona*, 212–13; Joseph C. McGowan, "A History of Long Staple Cotton," Thesis (University of Arizona, 1960); Smith, *Making Water Flow*, 185.

74. Haley, Interviews; Goodman, Interviews.

75. *Glendale News*, April 27, 1917, 1.

76. Ibid., March 30, 1917, 2.

77. Ibid., May 25, 1917, 1; Pat Richley-Erickson, "Age for WWI Draft Registration," *Dear Myrtle's Joy of Genealogy*, http://www.dearmyrtle.com.

78. Veronin, Fae Papin, *Molokans in Arizona* (Desert Hot Springs, CA: Self-published, 1999), 2–3; Sylvia Bender, "The Cultural Landscape of the Russian Molokan Colony, Glendale, Arizona," Manuscript (Arizona Historical Foundation, Arizona State University, 1976), 15.

79. *Glendale News*, June 8, 1917, 1.

80. Portnoy, "The Russian Molokans," 7.

81. *Glendale News*, November 2, 1917, 1; April 19, 1918, 4; April 26, 1918, 6.

82. Kluger, James R., *The Clifton-Morenci Strike: Labor Difficulty in Arizona, 1915–1916* (Tucson: University of Arizona Press, 1970).

83. David R. Berman, *Reformers, Corporations and the Electorate: An Analysis of Arizona's Age of Reform* (Newot: University Press of Colorado, 1992).

84. *Glendale News*, June 18, 1917, 1.

85. Portnoy, "The Russian Molokans," 7.

86. "Agreement for Sale of Real Estate," between John I. Chapman and Mary A. Chapman, and J.M. Haley, Arizona, October 16, 1917, Author's collection.

87. Haley, Interviews.

88. *Glendale News*, October 1, 1917; November 22, 1918, 2; McGowan, "A History of Extra Long Staple," 67; Smith, *Making Water Flow*, 190.

89. *Glendale News*, November 1917; December 28, 1917; January 11, 1918; January 18, 1918; January 25, 1918; February 1, 1918; February 8, 1918; March 15, 1918.

90. A. Truman Helm, "The Beginnings: From a Layman's Point of View," First Southern Baptist Church of Glendale, Arizona File, n.d., Arizona Baptist Historical Commission Archive; Martin, T.T. *The New Testament Church* (Kansas City, MO: Western Baptist, 1917); T.T. Martin, *Hell and the High Schools: Christ or Evolution, Which?* (Kansas City: Western Baptist, 1923).

91. Helm, "Beginnings," 4.

92. *Glendale News*, June 14, 1918, 3.

93. Ibid., May 1918; June 13, 1918, 2; Ollie Brooks, Rebecca Harris, Irma Deal, Photo, June 1918, Author's collection.

94. Bradford Luckingham, *Epidemic in the Southwest, 1918–1919* (El Paso, Texas: Texas Western Press, 1984).

95. *Glendale News*, October 25, 1918, 1; November 15, 1918, 3; Luckingham, *Epidemic*.

96. *Glendale News*, October 25, 1918, 1; November 8, 1918, 5; November 22, 1918, 1; Luckingham, *Epidemic*.

97. *Glendale News*, November 15, 1918, 3; December 20, 1918, 1; January 10, 1919, 1; January 24, 1919, 1; Luckingham, *Epidemic*.

98. Smith, *Making Water Flow*, 178–196; Sheridan, *Arizona*, 212–213; Receipts for payment, Joseph Haley by Glendale State Bank, Glendale, Arizona October 8, 1918, December 28, 1918, Author's collection.

99. *Glendale News*, November 28, 1919, 9; January 2, 1920, 4; McGowan, "A History of Long Staple," 67.

100. *Glendale News*, January 23, 1920, 1; Satisfaction of Mortgage between John I. Chapman and Mary A. Chapman and J.M. Haley, Arizona, 18 December 1919. Author's collection.

101. *Glendale News*, October 10, 1919, 2; June 1, 1920, 1.

102. Ibid., April 23, 1920, 1; May 21, 1920, 1; September 14, 1920, 1; September 18, 1920, 2.

103. Ibid., September 24, 1920, 2; October 22, 1920, 11; December 15, 1920, 6; January 8, 1921, 5.

104. Ibid., December 31, 1920, 6; January 8, 1921, 6.

Chapter 4

105. *Glendale News*, August 16, 1921, 1.

106. Ibid., March 12, 1920, 1.

107. Photo, Nannie and William Haley, circa 1920, Author's collection.

108. Genevieve Hannah, Interviews by the author, Tape recording (Youngtown, AZ): April 28, 2000; May 3, 2000; May 19, 2000; July 10, 2000.

109. *Glendale News*, January 12, 1922.

110. Hannah, Interviews; Varney Bible, Collection of Ruth Wilkinson.

111. Letter, Nannie Haley to Bessie Canter mentioning term "stork," December 27, 1925, Author's collection.

112. Haley, Interviews.

113. Ibid.

114. *Glendale News*, January 12, 1922, 5; June 1; 1922, 2; Principal note, Missouri State Life Insurance Company to Joseph M. Haley and Ollie G. Haley, Arizona, December 22, 1922; Satisfaction of Mortgage, executed by Joseph M. Haley, December 22, 1922, Author's collection.

115. R. Douglas Hurt, *Problems of Plenty: The American Farmer in the Twentieth Century* (Chicago: Ivan R. Dee. 2002), 43–46.

116. *Glendale News*, October 10, 1919, 2; June 15, 1920, 1; January 14, 1921, 2; November 24, 1921, 1; January 18, 1921, 6; May 12, 1921, 3; June 2, 1921, 1; November 24, 1921, 1; July 6, 1922, 6; February 2, 1923, 2; March 13, 1923, 2; July 6, 1923, 1; July 27, 1923, 1.

117. Ibid., January 14, 1921, 2; June 23, 1921. 2; April 19, 1921, 4.

118. *Arizona Republic*, April 30, 1923, 6; March 29, 1925, 9; December 5, 1925, 1; Michael J. Kotlanger, "Phoenix, Arizona: 1920–1940," Dissertation (Arizona State University, 1983), 23–24; Smith, *Making Water Flow*, 235–36.

119. *Wyoming v. Colorado*, 259 U.S. 466 Supreme Court (1922); John S. Goff, *George W.P. Hunt and His Arizona* (Pasadena, CA: Sociotechnical Publications, 1973); Walter Rusinek, "Against the Compact: The Critical Opposition of George W.P. Hunt," *Journal of Arizona History*, 25 (1984): 155-158; Norris Hundley Jr., *Water and the West: The Colorado River Compact and the Politics of Water in the American West,* 2nd edition (Berkeley: University of California Press, 2009) ix–xi, 110–132, 215–249; Sheridan, *Arizona*, 219–227.

120. *Glendale News*, January 21, 1921, 6; February 22, 1921, 4.

121. Ibid., August 30, 1920, 1; April 29, 1921, 5; May 12, 1921, 5; May 19, 1921, 1; July 14, 1921, 7; July 28, 1921, 1; August 4, 1921, 1; December 1, 1921, 2; March 16, 1922, 3; June 1, 1922, 4; February 16, 1923, 1; March 30, 1923, 3; *Arizona Republic*, April 24, 1923, 8.

122. *Glendale News*, March 22, 1921, 1; March 29, 1921, April 12, 1921, 1; April 15, 1921, 1; July 28, 1921, 1; May 5, 1922, 1.

123. Ibid., November 16, 1922, 3; Sheridan, *Arizona*, 215–216; Bradford Luckingham, *Minorities of Phoenix: A Profile of Mexican American, Chinese America, and African American Communities, 1860–1992* (Tucson: University of Arizona Press, 1994), 32.

124. *Glendale News*, April 12, 1921, 1; March 30, 1922, 1; November 16, 1922, 3.

125. Ibid., August 25, 1921, 5; December 15, 1921, 2; June 15, 1922, 4; First Baptist, "History."

126. *Glendale News* April 16, 1920, 1; May 18, 1920, 3; October 22, 1920, 1; December 28, 1920, 5; February 11, 1921, 1; July 14, 1921, 5.

127. Barry Hankins, *God's Rascal: J. Frank Norris and the Beginnings of Southern Fundamentalism* (Lexington: University Press of Kentucky, 1996), 22; Marsden, *Fundamentalism*, 153–69.

128. *Glendale News*, August 25, 1921, 5; December 15, 1921, 2; First Baptist, "History."

129. Ralph T. Bryan, "A History of First Southern Baptist Church, Phoenix, Arizona, 1921–1996," Manuscript (Phoenix: First Southern Baptist Church of Phoenix, circa 1996), 6–10; "A Word of Explanation" Pherne Peniger (re: founding of the first Glendale Southern Baptist Church), n.d., First Southern Baptist Church Glendale file, Arizona Baptist Historical Commission Archive.

130. Marsden, *Fundamentalism*, 166–69.

131. *Glendale News*, December 21, 1922, 8; January 30, 1923, 1; Charles C. Alexander, *The Ku Klux Klan in the Southwest* (Norman: University of Oklahoma Press, 1965).

132. *Dunbar's* (Phoenix, AZ), May 27, 1922, 3; September 29, 1923,4; *Glendale News,* January 29, 1923, January 30, 1923, 10; October 26, 1923, 1; *Arizona Republic*, April 24, 1923, 1.

133. *Glendale News*, May 7, 1924, 10; May 21, 1924, 1; *Dunbar's*, May 24, 1924, 4; May 31, 1924, 3; June 14, 1924, 5; September 6, 1924, 6.

134. *Glendale News*, September 14, 1923, 2; February 5, 1925, 1; *Arizona Republic*, March 23, 1925, 10.

135. *Glendale News,* July 9, 1924, 1; July 16, 1924, 1.

136. LouEdna McAllister, Interviews by author, Tape recording (Glendale, AZ): June 2, 2000; February 5, 2001.

137. Ibid.

Chapter 5

138. Wikipedia, "Gila River," *Wikipedia*, http://en.wikipedia.org/wiki/Gila_River.

139. Christine Pfaff, "Historic American Engineering Record, San Carlos Irrigation Project," Bureau of Reclamation (1996), 5–13; Zarbin, *Roosevelt Dam*, 30, 51–52; Sheridan, *Arizona*, 217–18: Wikipedia, "Pima people," *Wikipedia*, http://en.wikipedia.org/wiki/Pima_people.

140. Pfaff, "Historic American," 15–18.

141. *Northside News* (Glendale, AZ), October 12, 1925, 3; December 17, 1925, 1; Satisfaction of Mortgage Joseph M. Haley and Ollie G. Haley to Missouri State Life Insurance Company, December 23, 1925, Author's collection.

142. *Arizona Republic*, April 11, 1925, 1; April 14, 1925, 12; *Northside News*, July 9, 1925, 1.

143. Letter, Nannie Haley to Bessie Canter, December 27, 1925, Author's collection.

144. Haley, Interviews.

145. Haley, Interviews; Edward J. Larson, *Summer for the Gods: The Scopes Trial and America's Continuing Debate Over Science and Religion* (New York: Basic Books, 1997), 123–27; Martin, *Hell and the High Schools*; First Baptist, "History."

146. Reverend Ed G. Butler to First Baptist Church, Glendale, February 7, 1926, First Southern Baptist Church, Glendale (formerly Calvary Southern Baptist Church) file, Arizona Baptist Historical Commission Archive.

147. *The Doctrinal Trumpet,* March 28, 1926; April 1926, First Southern Baptist Church, Glendale file, Arizona Baptist Historical Commission Archive.

148. *Arizona Republic,* April 28, 1925, no. 2, 6; *Northside News,* March 4, 1926, 1; March 13, 1926, 1; March 28, 1926, 1; April 29, 1926, 1; May 6, 1926, 1; May 13, 1926, 1; May 20, 1926, 6; Eddie Pullins, "The Glendale Greys," March 15, 1993, Meeting Tape, Glendale Historical Society Archives; Arizona Interscholastic Association. "Arizona High School Baseball Records." *Arizona Interscholastic Association.* http://www.aiaonline. org/files/237/baseball-records.pd.

149. *Arizona Republic,* April 30, 1925, 2; Goodman, Interviews.

150. William J. Barber, *From New Era to New Deal: Herbert Hoover and American Economic Policy, 1921–1933* (New York: Cambridge University Press, 1985), 1–72; Hurt, *Problems of Plenty,* 17–25, 38–44, 57-62; Arizona Academy, *Tenth Arizona Town Hall, Do Agricultural Problems Threaten Arizona's Total Economy?* (University of Arizona, 1966–67), 55.

151. *Northside News,* December 2, 1926, 1; Quitclaim Deed, Joseph M. Haley and Ollie G. Haley to William M. Haley and Nannie R. Haley, March 6, 1926, Phoenix.

152. *Northside News,* March 24, 1927, 1; July 14, 1927, 1; Arizona Academy, *Town Hall,* 36.

153. Haley, Interviews.

154. McAllister, Interviews.

155. *Northside News* September 6, 1927, 1.

156. Goodman, Interviews.

157. *Northside News* January 6, 1927, 1; Goodman, Interviews.

158. Goodman, Interviews.

159. *Casa Grande Valley News* (Case Grande, AZ), October 7, 1927, 1; Trekell, Marty, "A History of Casa Grande," file, Casa Grande Valley Historical Museum; Ruth Wilkinson, Interviews by author, Tape recording (Glendale, AZ): April 13 200; April 26; May 15.

160. Erik-Anders Shapiro, "Cotton in Arizona: A Historical Geography," Thesis (University of Arizona, 1989), 62; Pat H. Stein, "Homesteading in Arizona, 1862–1940: A Component of the Arizona Historic Preservation Plan," Arizona State Historical Preservation Office (Phoenix: AZ, 1990), 5; Sheridan, *Arizona,* 217–218; Wilkinson, Interview.

161. *Arizona Blade Casa Grande Dispatch* (Casa Grande, AZ), May 3, 1928, 1.

162. P.G. Spilsbury, "Wanted 25,000 Families," Coolidge Dam Edition, *Arizona Blade Casa Grande Dispatch and Bulletin*, May 1928, 17; Carlton, Mrs. Keith ("Mickey"), "Optimists in a Desert Paradise," *Casa Grande Valley Historical Society Bi-Centennial Monograph*, 3, 1977.
163. Hundley, *Water and the West*, 215–81; Sheridan, *Arizona*, 223; Goff, *George W.P. Hunt*, 242, 245, 253.
164. Wilkinson, Interviews.
165. *Northside News* February 20, 1928, 1; July 3, 1928, 1; July 24, 1928, 1; December 25, 1928, 1; *Glendale News* May 4, 1929, 11; September 17, 1929, 1; October 25, 1929, 1.
166. McAllister, Interviews.
167. *Glendale News*, July 26, 1929, 1; September 17, 1929, 1; October 25, 1929, 1.
168. Wilkinson, Interviews.
169. Pinal County Land Transactions, Book 50, Varney, Leo J. et ex. to H. B. Gray et ex et al. June 27, 1932.
170. Goodman, Interviews.
171. McAllister, Interviews.

Chapter 6

172. *Glendale News*, May 6, 1921, 5.
173. *Northside News*, September 6, 1927, 1.
174. *Glendale News*, December 17, 1929, 1; April 30, 1930, 1; July 3, 1930, 1; January 1, 1931, 4.
175. Barber, *From New Era*, 72–100; Hurt, *Problems of Plenty*, 62.
176. Goodman, Interviews.
177. Barber, *From New Era*, 72–92; Hurt, *Problems of Plenty*, 62; Goodman, Interviews.
178. Goodman, Interviews.
179. *Glendale News*, July 23, 1930, 1; December 10, 1930, 1; January 29, 1931, 1.
180. Ibid., January 8, 1931, 1; Haley, Bible, Author's collection.
181. Haley, Interviews.
182. Wilkinson, Interviews.
183. *Glendale News*, February 15, 1935, 1; March 22, 1935, 5; November 22, 1935, 3; Arizona Baptist Historical Commission Archive, April 3, 1936, 1.

184.*Glendale News*, May 7, 1931, 2; June 11, 1931, 1; April 7, 1932, 1; October 14, 1932, 1; November 2, 1934, 6; David M. Kennedy, *Freedom from Fear: The American People in Depression and War: 1919–1945* (New York: Oxford University Press, 1999), 69, 76; Kotlanger, "Phoenix, Arizona," 255; William S. Collins, *The New Deal in Arizona* (Phoenix: Arizona State Parks Board, 1999), 24.

185. Raymond Moley, *The First New Deal* (New York: Harcourt, Brace and World, 1966), 272–282; Collins, *New Deal*, 25; Barber, *From New Era*, 22–32.

186. Moley, *The First New Deal*, 128; Haley, Interviews.

187. *Glendale News*, December 23, 1933, 8; Arizona State Board of Health, Certificate of Death for Margaret K. Brooks, March 9, 1932. Maricopa County, Arizona.

188. *Glendale News*, March 3, 1933, 1; March 17, 1933, 1,4; March 31, 1933, 1; May 19, 1933, 1; April 7, 1933, 2; June 30, 1933, 1; July 14, 1933, 1; August 25, 1933, 1; September 8, 1933, 1.; Kennedy, *Freedom from Fear*, 146–159.

189. *Glendale News*, August 20. 1932, 1; Haley, Interview.

190. Kennedy, *Freedom from Fear*, 140–144, 177, 200; Hurt, *Problems of Plenty*, 70–95.

191. Collins, *The New Deal*, 186.

192. *Glendale News*, May 19, 1933, 2; August 11, 1933, 5; August 25, 1933, 1; September 1, 1933, 2; September 15, 1933, 6; Collins, *The New Deal*, 190, 276; Hurt, *Problems of Plenty*, 70–73, 82; Frank Urtuguastegui, "The Farmworkers' Conditions in Arizona During the 1930," Manuscript, 1972. Library, Chicano Small Collection, Arizona State University.

193. Hannah, Interviews.

194. *Glendale News*, January 25, 1935, 6; Hannah, Interviews; Wilkinson, Interviews.

195. *Glendale News*, October 4, 1935, 1; February 1, 1936, 1; Collins, *The New Deal*, 58, 276; Kennedy, *Freedom From Fear*, 218.

196. *Glendale News*, December 13, 1935, 1; January 3, 1936, 1; Bureau of Reclamation, "Hoover Powerplant." *Bureau of Reclamation*, http://www.usbr.gov/projects/Powerplant.jsp?fac_Name=Hoover+Powerplant.

197. Hundley, *Water and the West*, 282–300.

198. *Glendale News*, August 2, 1935, 1; June 21, 1936, 1; May 14, 1937, 1; Kennedy, *Freedom from Fear*, 207; Kotlanger, "Phoenix Arizona," 25–56.

199. Haley, Interview.

200. Ibid.

201. For more on Elton Yancy, see: *Glendale News*, May 22, 1936, 1; May 28, 1937, 1. Girls softball: May 14, 1931, 3; April 26, 1935. Nearly every issue of the *Glendale News*, March-July carried news of some team.

202. McAllister, Interviews.

203. Wilkinson, Interviews.

204. Hannah, Interviews.

205. Letter from Phoenix Title and Trust Company to Joseph M. Haley referencing recent purchase, April 10, 1937, Author's collection.

206. *Glendale News*, May 29, 1936, 4; November 20, 1936, 1; June 12, 1936, 1; August 27, 1937, 1; April 1, 1938, 1; June 17, 1938, 1.

207. Urtuguastegui, "The Farmworkers," 3, 7; Haley, Interviews.

208. *Glendale News*, January 29, 1937, 1; May 28, 1937; June 11, 1937, 1; September 10, 1937, 1.

209. Ibid., September 17, 1937, 1; December 24, 1937, 1; July 8, 1938, 1.

210. Ibid., September 10, 1937, 1; Goodman, Interviews.

211. Haley, Interviews.

212. McAllister, Interviews.

213. Haley, Interviews.

214. Ibid.

215. Arizona Interscholastic Association, "Arizona High School Baseball Records," *Arizona Interscholastic Association*, http://www.aiaonline.org/files/237/baseball-records.pdf.

216. *Glendale News*, December 31, 1937, 2; June 17, 1938, 1; September 23, 1938, 1.

217. Joe Christy, and Jeff Ethell, *P-38 Lightning at War* (New York: Charles Scribners and Sons, 1978), 8–11; Goodman, Interview.

218. *Glendale News*, September 22, 1939, 2; November 10, 1939, 6; November 24, 24, 1939, 1.

219. Ibid., March 29, 1940, 1; January 10, 1941, 1; February 14, 1941, 1; March 7, 1941, 1.

220. Ibid., January 2, 1941, 1; March 13. 13, 1941, 1; Kennedy, *Freedom from Fear*, 524, 527; Christy, *P-38 Lightning at War*, 11; Stewart Wilson, *Zero, Hurricane and P-38* (Fyshwick, Australia: Aerospace Publications, 1996), 69–82; Edward Jablonski, *Airwar*, Vol. 3, "Book I Kenney's Kids"; Hill Air Force Base. P-38 'Lightning.'" *Hill Air Force Base.* http:///www.hill.af.mil/library/factsheets/factsheet.asp?=5662.

221. *Arizona Republic*, December 8, 1941, 7; December 9, 1941, 9.

222. *Glendale News*, March 6, 1942, 1; *Arizona Republic*, January 15, 1942, section 2, 1.

223. Roger Daniels, *The Decision to Relocate Japanese Americans* (New York: J.B. Lippincott Company, 1975), 43–49.

224. The intern Glendale Buddhist priest was considered a dangerous enemy alien and interred on direct order from Attorney General Francis Biddle; *Glendale News*, May 1, 1942, 1; *Arizona Republic*, December 10, 1941, 1; December 16, 1941, 7; December 18, 1941, 7, 8; December 21, 1941, 1; January 2, 1942, 1; January 15, 1941, section 2, 1; *Glendale News*, December 12, 1941, 1; Daniels. *The Decision to Relocate*, 3–5.

225. *Glendale News*, February 13, 1942, 5; February 20, 1942, 2; May 1, 1942, 2; January 1, 1943, 1.

226. Ibid., September 28, 1942, 1; Smith, *Making Water Flow*, 275–276.

227. *Glendale News*, January 6, 1942, 8; August 27, 1942, 2; September 26, 1942, 5; March 5, 1943, 1; Kennedy, *Freedom from Fear*, 777.

Chapter 7

228. Haley, Interviews.

229. Jean Provence, "History of the 3600th Flying Training Wing (Fighter), Luke Air Force Base," Manuscript, Library (Phoenix: Arizona State University, 1954), 1.

230. Haley, Interviews.

231. George W. Barr, *Bulletin*, # 206 (Tucson: University of Arizona, 1947), 12; Haley, Interviews.

232. *Glendale News*, July 5, 1946, 1; January 25, 1946, 4; August 11, 1944, 4.

233. Ibid., March 15, 1946, 3

234. Ibid., June 14, 1946, 3; July 28, 1950, 1; April 12, 1952, 12.

235. Ibid., October 24, 1946, 3.

236. Spring Training Online, "1946–Present: Spring Training History," *Spring Training Online*, http://www.springtrainingonline.com/features/history-3.htm; Haley, Interviews.

237. Barr, *Bulletin*, #220, 1949; Haley, Interviews.

238. Barr, *Bulletin*, #220, #232, 1951.

239. *Glendale News*, August 10, 1951, section 2, 2.

240. Ibid., July 11, 1952, 1; November 28, 1952, 1.

241. Ibid., January 6, 1950, 1; Richard Craig, *The Bracero Program: Interest Groups and Foreign Policy* (Austin: University of Texas Press, 1971), 10, 65.

242. *Glendale News*, October 22, 1948, 1; February 23, 1951, October 31, 1952, 1; September 11, 1953, 1; January 1, 1954, 1; September 10, 1954, 1.

243. Ibid., January 3, 1952, no. 2, 3; August 6, 1952, 2.

244. Provence, "History of the 3600th;" George David Smith, *From Monopoly to Competition: The Transformation of Alcoa, 1888–1986* (New York: Cambridge University Press, 1988), 242–287; Ivan Saddler, "How Motorola Got to Arizona," *Southwest Museum of Engineering, Communications and Computation*, http://www.smecc.org/motorola___arizona.htm; Gerald Nash, *The American West Transformed: The Impact of the Second World War* (Lincoln: University of Nebraska Press, 1985), 14–35.

245. Barr, *Bulletins*, #220, 1949; 242, 251.

246. Senators Carl Hayden and Ernest W. McFarland as quoted in Hundley, *Water and the West*, 301.

247. Salt River Project Heritage, "A History of the Salt River Project," *Salt River Project Heritage*, http:// www.srpnet.com/about/history.

248. *Glendale News*, November 14, 1952, 1.

249. Ibid., April 20, 1951, section 2, 2; May 4, 1951, section 2, 6; December 5, 1951, 1; March 14, 1952, 1; September 5, 1952, 1; November 14, 1952, 1; November 21, 1952, 6; November 28, 1952, 1; John Harrison Akers, *From Dale to Hollow: The Urban Transformation of Glendale, Arizona, 1940–1990*, Thesis (Arizona State University, 1997), 106–114.

250. *Glendale News*, April 18, 1952, 2; September 19, 1952, section 2, 2; November 15, 1952, 1; November 21, 1952, 6; November 28, 1952, 1; April 3, 1953, 1; July 10, 1953, 1; December 11, 1953, 3; May 21, 1954, 1; June 4, 1954, 1; Regarding annexation: *Glendale News*, August 10, 1951, 1; September 7, 1951, 1; December 5, 1951, 1; September 18, 1954, 2; November 16, 1954, 1.

251. Alain L. Omstead and Paul W. Rhode, *Creating Abundance. Biological Innovation and American Agricultural Development* (New York: Cambridge University Press, 2008), 100, 165, 195, 330.

252. Akers, *From Dale*, 112–13.

253. Harold H. Martin, "The New Millionaires of Phoenix," *The Saturday Evening Post*, 30 (September 1961: 25–33.

254. Haley, Interview.

255. *Arizona v. California et al.*, 373 U.S. 564, 565 Supreme Court (1963).

BIBLIOGRAPHY

Interviews

Goodman, Ada Fern (née Bobbe). Interviews by author. Tape recording. Glendale, AZ: January 9, 2001; January 24, 2001; April 13, 2002.

Haley, Joe, Jr. Interviews by author. Tape recording. Glendale, AZ: February 28, 2000; March 20, 2000; April 17, 2000; April 28, 2000; July 12, 2000.

Hannah, Genevieve. Interviews by author. Tape recording. Youngtown, AZ: April 28, 2000; May 3, 2000; May 10, 2000; July 10, 2002.

McAllister, Louedna. Interviews by author. Tape recording. Glendale, AZ: June 2, 2000; February 5, 2001.

Wilkinson, Ruth. Interviews by author. Tape recording. Glendale, AZ: April 13, 2000; April 26, 2000; May 15, 2000.

Manuscripts

Bender, Sylvia. "The Cultural Landscape of the Russian Molokan Colony, Glendale, Arizona." Manuscript. Arizona Historical Foundation, Arizona State University, 1976.

Bryan, Ralph T. "A History of First Southern Baptist Church, Phoenix, Arizona, 1921–1996." Manuscript. First Southern Baptist Church of Phoenix, Circa 1996.

Cartwright School District. "100 Years of Quality Education, 1884–1984." Manuscript. Centennial Program, Cartwright School District, 1984.

Finerman, Sandy. "A History of Glendale Union High School District." Manuscript. Phoenix Public Library, 1978.

First United Methodist Church of Glendale, Arizona. "A Century in Mission and Ministry." Manuscript. 1994.

Holmes, Irene Cartwright. "History of the Cartwright Family." Notes. Phoenix Public Library, 1993.

Provence, Jean, "History of the 3600th Flying Training Wing (Fighter), Luke Air Force Base." Manuscript. Library, Arizona State University, 1954.

Urtuguastegui, Frank. "The Farmworkers' Conditions in Arizona During the 1930." Manuscript. Arizona State University Library, Chicano Small Collection, 1972.

Court Cases

Arizona v. California et al., 373 U.S. 564, 565 Supreme Court (1963).

Wyoming v. Colorado, 259 U.S. 466 Supreme Court (1922).

Newspapers

Arizona Blade Casa Grande Valley Dispatch (Casa Grande, AZ), 1928.

Arizona Gazette (Phoenix, AZ), 1898–1940.

Arizona Republic (Phoenix, AZ), 1904–2014.

Casa Grande Valley News (Casa Grande, AZ), 1927–28.

Dunbar's Weekly (Phoenix, AZ), 1914–26.

Glendale News (Glendale, AZ), 1905–24, 1928–60.

Northside News (Glendale, AZ), 1924–28.

Phoenix Enterprise (Phoenix, AZ), 1905–06.

Periodicals

Byrkit, James. "The Word on the Frontier: Anglo Protestant Churches in Arizona 1859–1899." *Journal of Arizona History* 21 (1980): 63–86.

Carlton, Mrs. Keith ("Mickey"). "Optimists in a Desert 'Paradise." *Casa Grande Valley Historical Society Bi-Centennial Monograph* 3 (1977).

Martin, Harold H. "The New Millionaires of Phoenix." *The Saturday Evening Post* 30 (September 1961): 25–33.

Rusinek, Walter. "Against the Compact: The Critical Opposition of George W.P. Hunt." *Journal of Arizona History* 25 (1984): 155–170.

Books, Dissertations and Theses

Akers, John Harrison. "From Dale to Hollow: the Urban Transformation of Glendale, Arizona, 1940–1990." Thesis, Arizona State University, 1997.

Alexander, Charles C. *The Ku Klux Klan in the Southwest*. Norman: University of Oklahoma Press, 1965.

Arizona Academy. *Tenth Arizona Town Hall, Do Agricultural Problems Threaten Arizona's Total Economy?* Tucson: University of Arizona, 1966–67.

Barber, William J. *From New Era to New Deal: Herbert Hoover and American Economic Policy, 1921–1933*. New York: Cambridge University Press, 1985.

Barrios, Frank M. *Mexicans in Phoenix*. San Francisco: Arcadia Publishing, 2008.

Berlage, Gai Ingham. *Women in Baseball: The Forgotten History*. Westport, CT: Praeger, 1994.

Berman, David R. *Reformers, Corporations and the Electorate: An Analysis of Arizona's Age of Reform*. Newot: University Press of Colorado, 1992.

Botham, Fay, and Sara M. Patterson, eds. *Race, Religion, Region: Landscapes of Encounter in the American West*. Tucson: University of Arizona Press, 2006.

Christy, Joe, and Jeff Ethell. *P-38 Lightning at War*. New York: Charles Scribners and Sons, 1978.

Collins, William S. *The New Deal in Arizona*. Phoenix: Arizona State Parks Board, 1999.

Craig, Richard. *The Bracero Program: Interest Groups and Foreign Policy*. Austin: University of Texas Press, 1971.

Daniels, Roger. *The Decision to Relocate Japanese Americans*. New York: J.B. Lippincott Company, 1975.

Goff, John S. *George W.P. Hunt and His Arizona*. Pasadena, CA: Sociotechnical Publications, 1973.

Griswold, Robert L. "Anglo Women and Domestic Ideology in the American West in the Nineteenth and Early Twentieth Centuries." In *Western Women: Their Land, Their Lives*. Edited by Lillian Schlissel, Vicki L. Ruiz and Janice Monk. Albuquerque: University of New Mexico Press, 1988.

Hankins, Barry. *God's Rascal: J. Frank Norris and the Beginnings of Southern Fundamentalism*. Lexington: University Press of Kentucky, 1996.

Hundley, Norris, Jr. *Water and the West: The Colorado River Compact and the Politics of Water in the American West.* 2nd ed. Berkeley: University of California Press, 2009.

Hurt, R. Douglas. *Problems of Plenty: The American Farmer in the Twentieth Century.* Chicago: Ivan R. Dee, 2002.

Hustad, Donald P. *Jubilate! Church Music in the Evangelical Tradition.* Carol Stream, IL: Hope Publishing Company, 1981.

Jablonski, Edward. *Airwar.* Vol. 3. New York: Doubleday, 1979.

Kennedy, David M. *Freedom from Fear: The American People in Depression and War: 1919–1945.* New York: Oxford University Press, 1999.

Kluger, James R. *The Clifton-Morenci Strike: Labor Difficulty in Arizona, 1915–1916.* Tucson: University of Arizona Press, 1970.

Kotlanger, Michael J. "Phoenix, Arizona: 1920–1940." Dissertation, Arizona State University, 1983.

Kravetz, Robert E., and Alex Jay Kimmelman. *Healthseekers in Arizona.* Phoenix, AZ: Academy of Medical Sciences of the Maricopa Medical Society, 1998.

Larson, Edward J. *Summer for the Gods: The Scopes Trial and America's Continuing Debate over Science and Religion.* New York: Basic Books, 1997.

Luckingham, Bradford. *Epidemic in the Southwest, 1918–1919.* El Paso: Texas Western Press, 1984.

———. *Minorities of Phoenix: A Profile of Mexican American, Chinese American and African American Communities, 1860–1992.* Tucson: University of Arizona Press, 1994.

Marsden, George M. *Fundamentalism and American Culture: The Shaping of Twentieth-Century Evangelism, 1870–1925.* New York: Oxford University Press, 1980.

Martin, T.T. *Hell and the High Schools: Christ or Evolution, Which?* Kansas City, MO: Western Baptist, 1923.

———. *The New Testament Church.* Kansas City, MO: Western Baptist, 1917.

Mawn, Geoffrey P. "Phoenix, Arizona: Central City of the Southwest, 1870–1920." Dissertation, Arizona State University, 1979.

McGowan, Joseph C. "A History of Long Staple Cotton," Thesis, University of Arizona, 1960.

Mijakawa, T. Scott. *Protestants and Pioneers: Individualism and Conformity on the American Frontier.* Chicago: University of Chicago Press, 1964.

Moley, Raymond. *The First New Deal.* New York: Harcourt, Brace and World, 1966.

Morgan, Robert J. *Then Sings My Soul: 150 of the World's Greatest Hymn Stories.*

Nashville: Thomas Nelson Press, 2003.

Nash, Gerald. *The American West Transformed: The Impact of the Second World War*. Lincoln: University of Nebraska Press, 1985.

Nevins, Allan, and Henry Steele Commager and Jeffrey Morris. *Pocket History of the United States*. New York: Simon and Schuster, 1992.

Omstead, Alain L., and Paul W. Rhode. *Creating Abundance: Biological Innovation and American Agricultural Development*. New York: Cambridge University Press, 2008.

Pry, Mark E. "Arizona and the Politics of Statehood, 1889–1912." Dissertation, Arizona State University, 1995.

Sellers, William D., and Richard H. Hill and Margaret Sanderson-Rae, eds. *Arizona Climate: The First Hundred Years*. Tucson: University of Arizona, 1985.

Shapiro, Erik-Anders. "Cotton in Arizona: A Historical Geography." Thesis, University of Arizona, 1989.

Sheridan, Thomas E. *Arizona: A History*. Tucson: University of Arizona Press, 1995.

Smith, George David. *From Monopoly to Competition: The Transformation of Alcoa, 1888–1986*. New York: Cambridge University Press, 1988.

Smith, Jared. *Making Water Flow Uphill: The History of Agriculture in Mesa, Arizona*. Mesa, AZ: Mesa Historical Society: 2004.

Smith, Karen L. *The Magnificent Experiment: Building the Salt River Reclamation Project, 1890–1917*. Tucson: University of Arizona Press, 1986.

St. Clair, Carol J. Coffelt, and Charles S. St. Clair. *Glendale: Images of America*. Charleston, SC: Arcadia Publishing, 2006.

Szasz, Ferenc M. *Religion in the Modern American West*. Tucson: University of Arizona Press, 2000.

Veronin, Fae Papin. *Molokans in Arizona*. Desert Hot Springs, CA: Self-published, 1999.

Ware, Harry David. "Alcohol, Temperance and Prohibition in Arizona." Dissertation, Arizona State University, 1995.

Whitaker, Matthew. "In Search of Black Phoenicians: African American Culture and Community in Phoenix, Arizona, 1868–1940." Thesis, Arizona State University, 1997.

Wilson, Stewart. *Zero, Hurricane and P-38*. Fyshwick, Australia: Aerospace Publications, 1996.

Worster, Donald. *Rivers of Empire: Water, Aridity and the Growth of the American West*. New York: Pantheon Books, 1985.

Ynfante, Charles. *The Transformation of Arizona into a Modern State: The*

Contribution of War to the Modernization Process. New York: Edwin Mellen, 2002.

Zarbin, Earl A. *Roosevelt Dam: A History to 1911.* Phoenix: Salt River Project, 1984.

———. *Salt River Project: Four Steps Forward, 1902–1910.* Phoenix: Salt River Project, 1995.

———. *Two Sides of the River: Salt River Valley Canals, 1867–1902.* Phoenix: Salt River Project, 1997.

Archives

Arizona Baptist Historical Commission Archive

Casa Grande Valley Historical Society Museum

First Baptist Church, Glendale, Arizona files

Glendale Arizona Historical Society Archives

Reports and Other Published Information

Barr, George W. Bulletins, No. 206, 220, 232, 245, 252, 261, 270, 281, 292. Agricultural Experiment Station. Tucson: University of Arizona, 1947–1958.

Bureau of the Census. "Schedule No. 1-Population." Township 2N, Range E. In *Arizona Decennial Census Population in Retrospect.* Maricopa County, AZ, 1900.

Cartwright School District No. 83. "Centennial Program." Phoenix, AZ: April 14, 1984.

Central United Methodist Church, Phoenix, Arizona. "A Brief History." Central United Methodist Church. May 15, 2006. www.centralumc.com.

Pfaff, Christine. "Historic American Engineering Record, San Carlos Irrigation Project." Bureau of Reclamation, 1996.

Phoenix and Maricopa County Board of Trade. "Publicity Series." Circa 1900–1907. Phoenix: Arizona State Archives.

Stein, Pat H. "Homesteading in Arizona, 1862–1940: A Component of the Arizona Historic Preservation Plan." Arizona State Historical Preservation Office. Phoenix: 1990.

Territory of Arizona. "Report of the Superintendent of Public Instruction, 1898–1900."

Internet Files

Arizona Interscholastic Association. "Arizona High School Baseball Records." *Arizona Interscholastic Association.* http://www.aiaonline.org/files/237/baseball-records.pdf.

Bureau of Reclamation. "Hoover Powerplant." *Bureau of Reclamation.* http://www.usbr.gov/projects/Powerplant.jsp?fac_Name=Hoover+Powerplant.

Hill Air Force Base. "P-38 'Lightning.'" *Hill Air Force Base.* http:///www.hill.af.mil/library/factsheets/factsheet.asp?=5662.

Noon, Kathleen. "Industry Came to Glendale: Sugar Beet Factory History, Glendale, AZ: 1903–1910." http://www.molokane.org/molokan/Locations/Americas/Arizona/Noon.htm.

Portnoy, Esta, "The Russian Molokans: Glendale's Spirited Immigrants," 1981. http://molokane.org/molokan/Locations/Americas/Arizona/Portnoy/.

Richley-Erickson, Pat. "Age for WWI Draft Registration," *Dear Myrtle's Joy of Genealogy.* http://www.dearmyrtle.com.

Saddler, Ivan. "How Motorola Got to Arizona." *Southwest Museum of Engineering, Communications and Computation.* http://www.smecc.org/motorola___arizona.htm.

Salt River Project Heritage. "A History of the Salt River Project." *SRP Heritage.* http:// www.srpnet.com/about/history.

Spring Training Online. "1946–Present: Modern Spring Training History." *Spring Training Online.* http://www.springtrainingonline.com/features/history-3.htm.

Wikipedia. "Gila River." *Wikipedia.* http://en.wikipedia.org/wiki/Gila_River.

———. "Newlands Reclamation Act." *Wikipedia.* http://en.wikipedia.org/wiki/Newlands_Reclamation_Act.

———. "Pima people." *Wikipedia.* http://en.wikipedia.org/wiki/Pima_people.

INDEX